P9-DFL-625

STOP ARGUING & START NEGOTIATING

Strategies to Deal Effectively with Your Child

THE 3 STRATEGIES: ASK QUESTIONS, THINK OUT LOUD, TELL STORIES

JAMES F. MCTAMNEY, PhD

ISBN: 149235905X
ISBN 13: 9781492359050
Library of Congress Control Number: 2014916201
CreateSpace Independent Publishing Platform
North Charleston, South Carolina

CONTENTS

To Mark and Alise, who lived it with me.

Introduction

WHY THE 3 STRATEGIES TO NEGOTIATION PROGRAM?

In 1992, a film titled *A River Runs Through It*, which has relevance to the topic of negotiation, was released. An adaptation of the classic autobiography of Norman McLean, the film follows the lives of two young men coming of age in the 1900s. Raised in a strict Presbyterian household by their minister father, the young men grow up within the rigid structure and discipline imposed upon them.

Early in the film, an incident occurs that defines the character of the younger boy, Paul. He defies his father by refusing to eat a bowlful of oats. Paul's father reacts by saying that grace will not be said until the bowl is empty. The family leaves the table and the eight-year-old boy with the uneaten bowl of food. A power struggle ensues. Paul sits at the table but does not eat. The scene continues to show the standoff as time passes—the boy at the table; the father sitting in his study, looking out the window. As the clock on the wall reads 12:15 a.m., we see young Paul still sitting at the table with his food uneaten as the family gathers once again.

After all are seated, the father rises and announces that grace will be said. The meal proceeds with no mention of the previous rebellion. This entire sorrowful confrontation is a classic example of a parent falling into a trap of his own making without the awareness to resolve the issues. It is a painful scene I have seen played out in my office many times as a family grapples with power struggle issues. The focus of sessions with parents is to learn alternative ways to achieve their goals in a mutual, respectful way that builds self-esteem through negotiation.

Why would a parent need to negotiate with a child? At the outset, it may seem strange to write a parent-child book that emphasizes the need for negotiation. It may seem like common-sense wisdom that the parent gives orders and the child obeys. All too often, however, that is not quite the way it works. While the parent can give orders with the expectation that the child will comply, situations can frequently deteriorate into a full revolt.

Like it or not, your life is filled with parent-child negotiations that go on every day. Everything is a negotiation ranging from what the child will or will not eat for breakfast to establishing bedtime and whether or not a computer or video game can be taken to bed. These issues are just the beginning as other age-appropriate issues take their place (homework, grades, dating, parties, alcohol, social networking, cell phone usage…the list is endless).

As your child grows older, the need for increased independence grows. Parental lectures turn into shouting matches. Soon the family dog learns to take cover under a table as battles erupt. How many times have we all heard these familiar words from a parent, exhausted from arguing with a teenager: "I try to pick my battles." As a child's need for freedom grows and a parent's control diminishes, negotiation becomes a necessity rather than an option. You can start the process of negotiation now or wait until it is a must.

It is never too soon to teach negotiation skills—and, it's never too late. As you read through this book, you will see a good deal of the work is associated with parents and children. Despite that, this isn't strictly a parent-child guide because the principles of negotiation can be applied to almost any situation. When I'm teaching parents and couples how to negotiate, they have often reported back that the skills they learn translate to all sorts of other encounters. People actually say things like, "You know, this works in business, too." And why not? The principles that make for successful negotiation are applicable to many seemingly different situations, because the principles of negotiation are universal.

It is only logical that teaching good negotiation skills should begin in childhood. One of the things that is apparent in teaching parents how to deal with children is that they need to learn how to negotiate, not just give orders. Now, that may seem strange since it's obvious a parent is supposed to be the one in charge. So why do you have to learn how to negotiate? The answer is quite simple: negotiation skills will make life a good deal easier for everyone, especially for you and your children. After all, you give them lessons in many other things—swimming, sports, and dance. So why not negotiation?

Emphasis on Thinking Through Issues

Negotiation places an emphasis on the fundamental ability of the child to think through and problem-solve issues. This can be achieved through learning the 3 Strategies, which place the fundamentals of successful negotiation within reach of parent and child.

Emphasis is also placed on creating an environment in which the child is able to learn that ultimately positive behavior is its own reward. This may take an investment of time in the beginning. The focus of the 3 Strategies is away from the more passive behavior model in which something is done to the individual. This model views the subject more as a thinking and developing individual who is capable of making smart choices.

Roots of the 3 Strategies to Successful and Caring Negotiation

Stop Arguing & Start Negotiating incorporates the principles of cognitive behavior therapy with family and communication principles built upon the work of Milton Erickson. Central to this model is the concept that the child must first see *society's values rewarded.* Whether or how a specific behavior is to be rewarded is ultimately resolved by asking the question as to how the "mature world" views the situation. The goal is to teach a child what is expected by the world outside of the protective environment of the family—and to instill values that maximize the free choice of the child to behave appropriately.

In an effort to put the techniques described here within the reach of all, my experience has led me to firmly believe that learning and employing the 3 Strategies in communication can successfully accomplish it.

To Become a Good Negotiator You Must Learn to:

- Ask questions and wait for answers. (Do not lecture.)
- Think out loud when considering options. (Outline all sides of an issue while thinking out loud.)
- Tell stories to reframe a dilemma. (People love stories. That's why movies are so popular.)

Why Is It Important to Use the 3 Strategies Approach?

It is important because the child is anything but passive. The 3 Strategies Approach to negotiation is based on asking questions, telling stories, and thinking out loud to involve the whole person in the process of behavioral change. Rather than viewing the subject as a passive recipient—he is not and will not be simply passive—the child is actively participating and learning through the interaction skills that are needed to develop a responsible sense of independence and accountability.

3 Strategies Negotiation attempts to build on many of the communication principles identified as the Palo Alto Approach and simplifies these approaches designed to creating changes. With effective negotiation, the method used is as valuable as the message one hopes to transmit.

Premises of the 3 Strategies to Successful Negotiation:

- Problems are not causes to withdraw from life; problems are *challenges for personal growth.*
- Failure is only failure if we treat it as such; failure is a *chance to learn, to overcome and to succeed.*
- Success does not often come easily; success comes through *consistent and systematic effort.*
- Growth does not happen when one focuses on others and asks them to change; growth is achieved by *recognizing and taking responsibility for one's own behavior.*

Complicating Factors

The challenge with trying to teach people how to negotiate effectively is complicated by many factors, not the least of which is the emotional component. Negotiating sounds so easy when it is explained in an intellectual format—a problem is outlined, a solution is formulated calmly and rationally…and the answer becomes apparent. But, in an actual situation, when there is no one to guide the process and two people may well become combatants—it can quickly become far more complicated. If emotions take over, someone may well begin to act out her feelings in negative behaviors and circumstances can escalate out of control.

The important thing to do when emotions run high is to stay in control while thinking through solutions. What you will read here is my attempt to break down some complex ideas and make them as straightforward and uncomplicated as possible. Despite what may appear to be simple directives at times, this book is intended to examine *how and why some interventions work*, rather than just give the directive ("Here is what to do…"), which many self-help books on child rearing tend to do. While *Stop Arguing & Start Negotiating* includes many common situations and suggested strategies to deal with those situations, it is not written as a precise "recipe book" to cover and resolve a specific crisis with your child. The purpose of *Stop Arguing & Start Negotiating* is to go beyond a present situation in an attempt to help you understand why and how the techniques expressed here will work. It is intended to help you become a better negotiator and, as you model the behavior, by extension, your child also will become a better negotiator.

It is important to make your child aware of the concern that underlies your rules because fundamentally the boundaries set by the parent are motivated by caring. Directions that are frequently given indirectly are intended to promote the serious business of teaching social values and skills. Negotiation is not a case of getting a "one-up" on the other guy. The purpose is not to *win*—this implies someone loses—but rather to create changes that will enable your child to grow and succeed in life.

Chapter 1

BUILDING A BLUEPRINT FOR SUCCESS—THE FIRST STRATEGY: ASK QUESTIONS, DON'T LECTURE

When a parent gives a direction to a child and the child obeys, the parent is happy and there are no grounds for conflict. Suppose, however, the parent gives a direction and the child simply does not obey. For example, what happens when the parent tells the child to turn off the computer or the TV to get ready for dinner and the direction is ignored? What is a parent to do? Repeat the direction? State the direction more emphatically while perhaps raising one's voice? And if you think being ignored is bad enough, what happens if the child begins to argue back by asking a series of challenging "why" questions? What happens next?

Well, the parent can explain the rationale. However, if a parent starts giving explanations of why directions should be obeyed, the parent is ceding control of situations to the child.

A fundamental principle in communication is whoever is asking the questions is in charge and whoever has to answer the questions is clearly not in charge. After a few exchanges of "why" or "why not," the parent is likely to say, "Just do it!" and the reason is "Because I told you to do it!" Continued lack of compliance on the part of the child is likely to escalate the situation and result in a parental lecture.

What happens when a parent begins to lecture? If the child does not appear to be paying attention, the lecture grows louder and longer as though sheer force of volume and number of words will win out. After a few minutes, the child's eyes glaze over as he begins to tune out what is being said, to the increasing upset of the parent. The child may also shrug and utter a bored, "Whatever," further upsetting the parent. At the conclusion of a lecture, the parent frequently asks in a raised voice, "Do you hear me?" Do you understand? Look at me." As a last resort, the parent can order the child, "Go to your room." Even if the child complies and goes to his room, this apparent victory can be lost should the door be slammed as a final unspoken word of defiance. If not handled correctly, the confrontation that began as a simple direction has become something far larger. It is no longer an interaction between parent and child that grew into a one-sided lecture, possibly escalating to a parental rant—it can become a disaster. And the parent is losing.

Lectures Don't Often Work: Why Is That?
Lectures are not likely to work because they often produce a "pushback" effect on the part of the listener. When a child does not want to do something, he frequently stops listening while the parent is lecturing because he feels it is the same lecture he has heard many times before. Or the child starts to think of reasons not to believe what the parent is saying. Hearing a familiar lecture, a child begins looking for inconsistencies and loopholes within the parent's directions to use when mounting an argument in his own behalf to avoid compliance.

When parents do not get the expected compliance from their children, the parental lecture usually becomes stronger and the tone more strident. The stronger the order becomes, the stronger the pushback effect on the part of the child. The same phenomenon occurs whenever any of us is subjected to a hard sell. As all of us know, anytime we are forced to listen to an overpowering sales pitch, the more we dislike the presentation and the more likely we are to resist what is being sold. A really hard and emphatic sales lecture by a parent is likely to produce the opposite from the intended effect. The harder the selling lecture, the greater the resistance grows.

Think back to the last disagreeable lecture you heard. After a while, you probably did not remember *what* was being said but you most likely remember *how* it was being said. It is similar to the basic idea that in conveying a message, 90 percent of the effectiveness is found in *how we look* and *how we sound*—and only 10 percent in *what we have to say.*

Who has not had the experience of listening to a sales pitch from a hard seller and, because of the style of presentation, found resistance grow until all the listener wanted to do was escape? The listener frequently does not change his mind and, in fact, comes away more convinced of the original position he held before the lecture began.

If lectures don't work well, why do so many people chose them as an option? And what is the resistance to giving up on lecturing? Well, one of the great resistances to not lecturing anymore is the perceived time-saving effect the lecture has over engaging an audience. Because of the time saving, lectures tend to be viewed as efficient. As a lecturer, you can say what you want in a short span of time—and as a parent, you get to discharge your frustration at the same time. Even if the lecture doesn't work to produce the desired effect, you released some energy and that may make you feel good for a few minutes.

Quite simply, lectures do not work very well. If lectures worked, the world would be changed by the end of the day. Instead of lecturing, what would happen if a parent were to take a different approach and begin to ask questions? Suppose, for example, instead of repeating a direction to a noncompliant child, the parent were to ask the child why he does not want to comply? As we will see, this changes the nature of the confrontation, keeps the parent from losing it, and puts the child on the spot to explain his actions. Your heart will thank you for making the change.

The Objective to Asking Questions: Make Eye Contact, Ask Questions, and Wait for Answers

When your child refuses to cooperate, the answer to overcoming the refusal begins with trying to engage with the child and not talk at the child. What is the child's reason for noncompliance? The only way to discover what is going on is to ask questions.

Years ago when I started teaching high school, I was very much into the lecture mode and the only question I consistently asked was—"Do you understand?" I didn't have time—or I didn't think I had the time—to wait for excuses. As a result of my approach, I went nowhere fast.

For months, I struggled to get compliance with a few resistant children. My requests and lectures for improvement and cooperation were consistently ignored. When told they needed to do particular tasks—like turning in homework assignments or paying attention—the students would simply look at me without response.

Desperate to turn things around, I decided to try a different approach. (Instead of lecturing them, I would try to find out why they did not want to cooperate.) I began inviting resistant children to return to the classroom at the end of the day. When a student would arrive, I started asking questions and began waiting for answers. Instead of lecturing, I began listening.

I soon discovered that it is not just asking the right question that is important; it is also about having the patience to wait for answers. I began to realize that children frequently do not know why—or at least cannot put into words—the problem. Often, at the outset, a student would maintain a stony silence as though waiting for the inevitable lecture. If the child did not answer, I would suggest without the hint of any sarcasm, that he could think about it and we could meet again the following day. That offer frequently produced results and the child would begin speaking.

Getting the first answer from a student may not have addressed the motivation behind the child's uncooperative behavior. I learned that asking another question or a series of questions would guide the students and me to the point of resistance and eventually to the source of the real problem. Agreement frequently resulted and change in behavior most often occurred. I discovered this approach worked well in a diversity of populations. Learning this is important because it leads to a principle— once something is put into words, it can begin to be resolved. Conversely, if someone cannot put what he needs into words, no one can help him.

There was an interesting spin off effect from using this slower approach. For each successive student with whom I interacted, the result was the same and it worked faster each time. Why was that? It began working so well and so quickly that I did not immediately realize—until one of the students told me the answer— the children were coaching one another on how to "handle" me. They told one another, "Don't argue with him about what you did, just admit what you did, apologize and tell him how you will do it right in the future." While my initial reaction was one of surprise that they had figured me out, I became aware I had taught the students how to negotiate with me and that was not bad. It was definitely much more efficient!

Once your child answers a question, begin a back and forth dialogue that includes the listener. You must find out what the listener believes and the only way you can do that is to ask questions and wait for answers. I have counseled people about taking this step and the most frequent objection I get is: "It takes too long if I have to ask questions. I do not want to go through all of that. I just want my child to do what I'm telling him to do."

Well, it may be quicker to lecture than to ask questions and wait for answers but where has that gotten you? Are your children more likely to listen to your lectures than you are to listen to a hard sell from someone? A child may listen to your lectures, even politely nod his head, but not necessarily comprehend or agree with what you are saying. We know from neuroscience that lectures only engage part of the brain and not for a very long period of time. A lecture also makes the listener passive. We want the child to be active in this process. You won't know if the child is involved until you hear what he has to say.

The First Strategy: Learn How to Ask Questions
You may be thinking that you have been asking questions for years, so what do you have to learn about *how* to ask questions? Well, all questions are not alike. We need a special type of question here, one that has its historical roots more than two thousand years ago in the time of Socrates.

A prominent philosopher and teacher in Greece, Socrates developed a unique approach to teaching. Instead of lecturing his students, he initiated an interactive style that became known as the Socratic Method. Perhaps Socrates was tired of looking at the blank expressions on the faces of the students he lectured or maybe Socrates just believed he had a better idea. Whatever the reason, Socrates started a tradition in education that is still with us today.

The questions Socrates asked were not asked of the students in a judgmental fashion where you get the right or wrong answer; rather, the questions were intended to be open-ended and designed to draw out the other person's thinking. To be successful at this, the questions had to go in sequence and be asked in an information-seeking fashion, leading the subject from not knowing to enlightenment.

Avoid the "Gotcha" Question
A "gotcha" question is designed to trip up the other person. When it is used in a classroom, the goal is to catch the student who has not studied or who is not prepared. Unfortunately, it is often for the teacher's own amusement or the amusement of the

other students. The gotcha question is not designed to lead the other person from not knowing to knowledge.

When the gotcha is sprung, being tripped up surely will not amuse the person who has to answer the question. It is quite likely that the person upon whom the game is played will refuse to answer questions in the future. Even quite innocent questions may be seen as potential traps. What the gotcha question really teaches is defensiveness. Even worse, the person who was caught will learn the same technique—and how to play "gotcha back" with the questioner, as a form of reprisal.

Avoid the "Sandbagging" Question

"Sandbagging" is the process leading to the gotcha question. In the context of asking questions, think of it as a metaphor of walking someone along the beach with an empty sock in one hand and a handful of sand in the other. Each successive question is like pouring another handful of sand into the sock until finally the sock is filled, tied off at the top, and the victim is hit with it. Sandbagging questions most often asked of a child are: "Where did you go?" "Who were you with?" and "What did you do?

Now, there's nothing wrong with any of these questions if the question is meant to acquire information that the parent does not have. If the parent already knows the answers and the reason for asking questions is to trap the child, the child will learn to avoid answering questions altogether in the future. His or her answers to the above questions are likely to be: "Nowhere," "Nobody," and "Nothing," respectively.

Sandbagging questions create a lose-lose scenario and convey the message, "I don't believe or trust you." As a result, sandbagging must be avoided.

Avoid Sarcasm

Sarcasm is defined as a cutting remark meant to ridicule the other person. It often passes as humor—at least to the person who is being sarcastic and wants to pass off what is being said as a joke.

Sarcasm can be obvious and over-the-top. "Well, good for you, you finally got something right." Or sarcasm can be subtler: "Well, I guess I should be thankful. It took long enough but it looks like you finally got it right." Sarcasm can take the form of the questions: "Are you stupid or just trying to act stupid?" "Do you ever listen?" or "Do you have to be told over and over again every time?"

Sarcasm can be conveyed with a change in one's voice, such as speaking slowly as though the other person has difficulty understanding. "You look like you are listening and understand but then you go and do just exactly what you want." Regardless of whether it's obvious or subtle, sarcasm should be avoided.

Open-Ended Questions Should Be the Goal

By asking open-ended questions, you're trying to seek information and help your child to examine what is motivating him and what is holding him back from cooperative behavior. It is important to know what is valued and how a particular action is either consistent or inconsistent with the child's value system. Open-ended questions help the child think through decisions and examine what is likely to be the result of the choices he is about to make. Do you know the child's values? Is there a conflict between what the child claims to be his values system and a more immediate objective that appears to be inconsistent with those stated values?

This conflict over values often arises because many times the object valued is different from and/or opposed to the child's more fundamental stated value. By asking questions of the child, potential conflicts can be seen and addressed.

Let's look at an example: say, the issue of health. Who would not say health is important? However, when we discuss the object that the child might value, there can be a real conflict. We may say that the child values health and yet the object valued may be a cigarette or a drug. The challenge here is asking questions to help the individual understand how there is a contradiction between his *value system* and the *objects he values*. The parent can challenge the child by saying, "You told me you value your health and yet you want to smoke. I don't understand. How does smoking take care of your health?"

The purpose of asking questions is to get the child to examine his beliefs without him having to worry about being sandbagged by a gotcha question. Asking questions in such a way as to get at the child's values is also a confirmation of belief in the child. It says to the child, "I believe you have the ability and intelligence to work out smart solutions to what you must do for the future."

Get Out In Front with Your Questions

Let's start with an example. If someone were to walk up to you and ask, "Do you have any money with you?" what would be your first thought? The other person wants to borrow money. How much? Do I really want to let this person borrow money? All sorts of thoughts and questions would probably run through your mind because you do not know how much money is involved. All you're pretty sure of is that the other person wants money. So how do you answer? "I left my checkbook at home." "I never carry anything more than a dollar." Whatever you answer, it probably will be somewhat cautious and hesitant, if not guarded.

But suppose the person approaching you pulls out a five-dollar bill and asks, "Do you have five ones for a five-dollar bill? I need single dollars for the vending machine so I can buy coffee."

How do you avoid awkward situations? The answer is easy—*get out in front* on questions. State your purpose in asking your question before you ask the question. It completely changes a situation. No one has to guess at what the other person wants. You know what is involved because the other person has gotten out in front on the question and eliminated the need to guess at the follow-up question. Suppose someone was to approach you and ask, "Do you have a car with you today?" where does your mind go now? Does this person want to borrow my car? Does this person need a ride and if so, how convenient or inconvenient will that be for me? Once again, you may find yourself groping to find a socially appropriate but defensive answer. "Yes, but the car has been acting strangely. It stalls a lot in heavy traffic," or "Yes, but I have to get right home after work today."

But let's suppose the other person gets out in front on the question and says "I had to drop my car off at the shop down the road this morning. If you're going that way on your trip home, could I get a ride with you?" Now, the answer is still yes or no but it certainly does cut down on the mental gymnastics that you will have to do before you answer. There was no attempt to either play "gotcha" with you or "sandbag" you.

Chapter 1 Questions

Am I finding myself lecturing, or interested in asking questions?

Am I waiting for answers or am I talking before an answer?

Am I asking "trap questions"—using "gotcha," or "sandbagging?"

Am I staying away from sarcasm?

Am I asking open-ended questions?

Am I getting out in front on questions?

Chapter 2

THE SECOND STRATEGY: TELL STORIES TO REFRAME SITUATIONS

Storytelling has long been a part of therapeutic approaches to problem solving. Why? Because people love stories and stories lend themselves to illustrating the practical things in everyday life. We love movies and books about people and we learn from them in ways that are different from listening to lectures or being told what to do and what not to do. With stories, we become more fully engaged. Stories win out over formal lectures. We remember information better in the context of a story. Take for example, the definitions of words. We remember the meaning of words better if embedded in a story rather than just hearing the definition stated as a fact.

A Story Can Help Us Remember the Meaning of a Word

There is an expression that is commonly used to answer the question as to whether one has the qualifications to do a job competently. That expression is summarized in the word *vetted*. You might know that *vetted* means you've done a background check on someone to evaluate a person's competency. While that is its meaning, its origin is quite fascinating. The word goes back to the mid-seventeenth century and was originally a horse racing term. Centuries ago, in order to ensure fairness of a race and before the horses could be allowed to participate in the race, all the horses had to be checked for flaws by a veterinarian beforehand. A veterinarian would be called in to evaluate the health and soundness of the horse. If the horse was pronounced healthy, the horse could be entered in the race. If not, the horse was disqualified. Over time, the more colloquial abbreviation "vet" or "to be vetted" was used. People would simply ask, "Has the horse been vetted?" That is how the verb *vet* came into our language and developed over time and took on the general meaning of to check or to evaluate. Now, let's think about the origin of the word for a moment. Having heard that story, isn't it more likely that someone will remember the meaning of the word because of the background story?

Neuroscience: Stories Have an Impact on the Brain

Studies in neuroscience have shown us just how great the impact of a story can have on the brain. When we listen to a traditional classroom PowerPoint presentation using bullet points and slides, the left side of the brain, where language is processed, is activated. A lecture engages the left side—commonly called the logical side—of the brain. The brain is engaged, but for how long?

Studies show a person generally pays attention for anywhere between ten to twenty minutes before the brain needs to go on break. After a break, the brain reengages and focuses on the information. But what happens when a story is told? Brain scans show that the right side of the brain, the emotional side, is also activated; and the whole brain becomes engaged. We not only understand, we *feel* and understand. Because the story engages the listener, the listener turns a story into his own story. It becomes a part of him.

Stories Cross the Divide of Language and Culture

Stories touch everyone; they cross over continents, cultures, and ages. Think of a famous story, and then check to discover into how many languages it has been translated. We tell our own story all the time. At work, we tell coworkers how we spent the week-end—what we did and what we experienced. At home, married couples return from work with the stories of others. The day is recounted in story format with each person listening to hear incidents that highlight their partner's day. We come home to hear familiar questions: "What did you do today?" "Did anything exciting happen?" or "Did you have a good day?"

Stories Evoke Feelings

We watch movies on TV, read books at bedtime, and tell stories to our children to help them relax and fall asleep. We tell stories to evoke all sorts of feelings, to engross, excite, soothe, and amuse. Stories communicate ways to behave, teach values, and help us to understand complex social interactions. Stories arouse empathy in us and help us understand another person's point of view.

Stories take us into worlds of good and evil, of rightness, and even, at times, unfamiliar worlds and situations that scare us. Despite the fright these stories may evoke, we venture into this scary world under controlled circumstances, which allows us to feel a sense of control. They make it possible for us to think through scary situations and consider what we might do in a similar situation in reality. They allow us to laugh at the characters, identify with them, and even laugh at ourselves. Stories are so effective because listeners become engaged in the story and learn what to do in an indirect way without having to actually experience the painfulness of a situation.

Stories in the Business World Are Effective

The same insights gained from neuroscience regarding the use of stories are being utilized in the business world, affecting how business is done more effectively. Businesses have discovered that convincing someone of something is not done with statistics, charts and tables, or talking about some abstract situation that requires a response. What businesses have learned is the effectiveness of letting people tell their story to other people. In keeping with a previous example, when statistics alone are used, only the left side of the brain is activated.

Businesses have learned the importance of telling a story through the eyes and experiences of other people. Instead of quoting statistics about how many people choose or do not choose a product, the goal is to have people talk to people. How many famous people collect money by endorsing a product in an attempt to persuade others to do the same? It is not just about choosing the right person; it is about choosing someone who is popularly viewed as honest and credible.

Less Is More

Business success is not tied to telling a story about millions, thousands, or even hundreds of people. Success is tied to telling the story through the eyes of just a few people or even one person. Why do businesses do this? Because they have found that telling the story of one person is more likely to arouse empathy, whereas telling the story of thousands of people creates a sense of being overwhelmed. If the problem is too big, the more probable it is to overwhelm the listener. As an example, a listener is likely to become more engaged in a call for empathy if a picture of someone in need is added. A listener is much more likely to respond to a picture and letter from a child who is in need of food than they would be to respond to an entire nation of people who are starving. The listener can say. "I can help a small child; I can't help a whole nation." It's all about telling a story.

Stories Inspire and Teach Values to Your Child

How does the effect of the story about one person translate to an interaction between parent and child? When the child is engaged in the story, he is more likely to see things in a different and perhaps a new way. How can we create the need for justice with stories?

People learn about injustice by reading a book or seeing a film like *The Diary of Anne Frank*. They learn about the injustice done to millions through the eyes of one person. Seeing how one person is affected resonates with us. We experience fear and feel a sense of outrage that someone could be treated so badly, the way poor Anne Frank was treated. We are outraged at the obvious injustice.

People understand the horrors of the Civil War when they see such films as *Red Badge of Courage* or *Killer Angels*. We experience the horror and futility of war, not just read statistics on how many lives were needlessly wasted. Even horror films (and I'm not recommending them) designed with a teenage audience in mind have had beneficial effects. Teenagers have been known to report learning what to do when they are at home in a time of crisis. Children certainly should be learning what *not* to do.

Stories Are Effective Because They Are Indirect

Storytelling can be used to teach values and ethics. Precisely because stories are indirect, they allow children to learn without having to be confronted in a more direct way. Courage can be expressed in many ways. Just saying no can sometimes show courage. The story allows the child to look at people and situations with objectivity. Stories allow us to confront ourselves in a nonjudgmental, nonconfrontational way. It teaches us to think through situations.

Keep It Simple

Simple, uncomplicated stories are more effective than longer more complex stories. Simple stories are easier to understand and easier to remember. How simple is the *Peanuts* cartoon that tells the story of Charlie Brown trying to kick a football that Lucy is holding for him. "I won't pull it away this time, Charlie Brown," Lucy says. When trying to remind somebody of the likelihood that they cannot depend upon someone else who has consistently proved to be unreliable, all that needs be said is,

"Go ahead and kick the ball, Charlie Brown. I won't pull it away this time." A powerful message is contained in a simple cartoon.

In a similar way, there is the fable of the Scorpion and the Frog. The story is simple, a scorpion and frog meet on the bank of the stream and the scorpion asks the frog to carry him across on its back. The frog asks, "How do I know you won't sting me?" The scorpion replies, "Because if I do, I will die, too." Midway across the stream, the scorpion stings the frog. Knowing they will both die, the frog asks, "Why?" The scorpion then replies, "Because it's my nature." Once again, it is a short story and universally known as one that packs a powerful message. Whether we like the story or not, we remember it.

We Remember Stories More Than Rules

We tend to remember *stories* more than we remember *rules*. The listener to a story can gain knowledge and imagine new possibilities—and even more important, the listener is likely to remember the point to the story.

In *To Kill a Mockingbird*, there is a story within a story. The title itself captures the fate of the man who was to die, Tom Robinson. Early in the plot, Atticus Finch tells his young son about his father and what his father told him when giving Atticus his first gun. His father admonishes him "…never to kill a mockingbird because it would be a sin" to do so. Atticus is told that all mockingbirds do is "…sing their hearts out and make beautiful music for us to enjoy."

It is only later in the film, when Atticus must make a decision regarding the fate of the man who saved the lives of his children, that we understand the importance of those words. Atticus carefully ponders the right thing to do: Should he name Boo Radley—the man who killed the attacker of his children, and who probably saved their lives—as the person responsible for the death of the attacker? If he does name Boo as the man who killed the attacker, Boo will have to stand trial. And, while Boo would likely be found not guilty, how would he fare in a trial?

The sheriff reminds Atticus that it would be a sin to do anything that would hurt the man who saved his children. Scout, Atticus's daughter, echoes the sheriff's judgment by saying, "It would be like killing a mockingbird."

While *To Kill a Mockingbird* may be a fictional story rather than a real-life episode, the message is clearly one that resonates with people and points out the effectiveness of storytelling.

Tell Stories

Suppose you, as a parent, are confronted by that age-old problem of getting your child to clean his room. You have tried ordering, threatening, and various forms of pleading. Suppose you try a story and begin by saying something like, "I was talking to some parents the other day and an issue came up that we have often had to deal with in the past regarding getting your room cleaned up. Mrs. Smith told me how she and her daughter had worked things out. When Mrs. Smith could no longer stand it, instead of ordering her daughter to get her room cleaned they identified something that her daughter wanted to do, like going out with her friends over the weekend. Mrs. Smith let her daughter decide the time when the room would be cleaned as long as it was done an hour before the deadline they had agreed upon. That seemed like a sensible approach to the situation and it worked out for them, so I'm going to give you the same kind of choice. What would you like to earn in return for cleaning your room?"

Once your child tells you his room has been cleaned up— *this next part is very important*—when you go upstairs to meet with him, *do not show any sign of gloating* or *become sarcastic*. To do either will turn victory into defeat. Instead, look around the room and congratulate your child not only for the good job he has done but also for the good choice he made in getting the room straightened out.

All this can be achieved in a fashion that avoids making the parent sound condescending or triumphant. By examining both sides of an issue and coming to a solution, the parent creates the impression of thinking through the issue while examining the possible outcomes. After all, isn't this the goal you're trying to accomplish? You always want your child to understand the positive end result of an action.

Stay Positive

If you want a positive response, you must stay positive. Tell positive stories that contain positive solutions. Avoid telling negative stories that highlight the wrong way to do things. Stories should be about embracing life and choosing goals to succeed—not about avoiding challenges and running away.

The film *The Shawshank Redemption* is a story about a group of men in prison. It is about overcoming tremendous adversity, and learning how to get along and live in such a world. The main character succeeds against great odds and grows as a person in the process. We want him to grow, to overcome obstacles, and finally to embrace life as a free man. His moment of triumph is our moment of triumph.

When Giving Directions Be Positive and Engage the Emotions and the Whole Brain

We should want to tell people what they should do and avoid telling them what not to do. If you tell people only what not to do, they may know what you do *not* want, but they may also be stuck as to what you *want* them to do. Focus only on the smart and right thing. If we consistently do something incorrectly, that is what we are likely to do when faced with a stressful situation in which there is little time to consider alternatives.

Consider safety instructions—whether it is the rules for a fire drill in the workplace, or what to do in an emergency situation while on an airplane. Safety procedures are not left up to the individual. In the event of an emergency, there is no time to look for the card with the safety instructions or to search for the chart on the wall that denotes the exits. Stories about disasters create a visceral reaction in us. We see or hear about what happens to people trapped in elevators and learn that, in the event of a fire, we should not try to use the elevator but instead use the stairs.

A story or movie about pain and suffering engages the whole brain more emphatically than hearing or reading the rules of what to do in case of a fire. If this is so, why don't people take emergency situations more seriously? Unfortunately, the answer to that is tied up in denial—the thought that "It won't happen to me."

Every year, it seems, in almost every community, there is the inevitable car accident involving a recently graduated senior. Do people learn from a tragedy like a car accident involving a friend? Some undoubtedly do because the story affects them on an emotional level. Perhaps they realize that it could have been them.

Studies from neuroscience show that strongly felt emotions help us focus and remember. People remember not just the event but where they were when they heard it. Think about the World Trade Center tragedy. People remember it because of the emotional overlay. That's what stories do for us. Stories help us remember and feel the event all over again. The more relevant the story, the more likely it is to engage the emotions and the memory. We will remember stories long after half-heard lectures have been forgotten.

Chapter 2 Questions

Am I reframing situations by telling stories?

Do my stories inspire to overcome challenges?

Am I staying positive with my stories, not saying what should *not* happen but what *should* happen?

Chapter 3

THE THIRD STRATEGY: THINK OUT LOUD TO NEGOTIATE EFFECTIVELY

You may not think of yourself as someone who negotiates with your child. You may think you should not have to negotiate with him. The reality is that you are already engaged in negotiations with your child every day—from the time he gets up in the morning until the time he goes to bed at night. You negotiate with whom he plays, what kind of toothpaste he will use, or what kind of cereal he will or will not eat. You may wish you did not have to negotiate—but you do…and you will have to continue to do so.

Cooperating is defined as getting your child to do what you want him to do. Take a moment to think how many times and in how many ways you try to talk your child into cooperating. If your child does not cooperate, you may find yourself moving from politely asking for compliance, to pleading, to threatening, and eventually to punishing; all symptoms of a failed negotiation are a source of frustration. And depending on the age of your child the nature of the negotiation will undergo adjustment as he grows and matures.

Negotiation will move from the relatively simple to the more complex. You begin negotiating when you give a direction and it is not obeyed. From birth to seven years, negotiations are generally minimal and reduced to relatively simple conditional statements like, "If you do…(some specific behavior), then you will get…(some specific reward)." This process usually works with a young child. You are in charge. You are the person who rewards behaviors. You negotiate by offering a specific reward to obtain a specific behavior. "If you eat your vegetables, you can have dessert." A child at this young age is not likely to enter into any kind of more sophisticated behavior other than to say no to your request. As your child begins to struggle to become an independent person, he may well say no—a lot.

The situation is likely to change between the ages of eight to twelve years of age. Your child is getting wise to your ways and is in the process of learning how to deal with you more effectively. He may take the stance, "I'm not going to do it and you can't make me." although he may not state that aloud. Now, you can continue to order him, raise your voice, tell him you really mean it this time and threatened to use dire consequences if he still refuses. (More later on handling the refusal to comply.)

Situations change radically once a child reaches thirteen years of age. At this stage of development, in an attempt to overturn demands, children begin to use logic to challenge. You are told how unfair you are, and how all the other parents don't place outrageous demands on their children the way you do. Your child will demand to know why he cannot have what he wants. You can choose to take a strong parental position, "I'm the parent and you're the child and you're going to do what I tell you to do." If you choose this position, you may luck out and your child may cooperate well into the future. If you are reading this book, however, you are likely faced with an increasingly rebellious child. You may, over time, find yourself getting worn out and conclude that in the future, you'll "pick your battles."

Learn the Rules of Negotiation
If you need to negotiate, why not take a look at how it is done by professional negotiators and see if some of the principles can be applied at home? One of the more well-known books in the field is *Getting to Yes: Negotiating without Giving In* by Roger Fisher and

William Ury, and one of their central premises is that *like it or not, we are all negotiators.* They emphasize focusing on the issues and common interests while separating personalities from the situation to be resolved. There should be mutual gain—not a winner and a loser. Additionally, there should be some objective way of measuring results.

You may be thinking, *This is fine in the business world, but I'm talking about children.* Actually, the principles apply very well to families and parent-child interactions. This is where understanding your child's position and thinking aloud become very important. If the parent makes a decision solely from the position of authority and doesn't consider what the child's issue might be, the issue may be overlooked and a power struggle could result. Forget for a moment that you are the authority figure and think about yourself as a negotiator. As the negotiator you are going to help the child think through not just the issue at hand; you will also begin teaching the process and importance of negotiation. The purpose is to teach a method your child can use for life—the process of making good choices. Get away from the idea that your authority is being challenged and put yourself in a negotiator's mind-set. If you argue strictly from a "parent" position, there can be no negotiation and you will wind up in polarized positions. With negotiation, two things result:

1. You avoid a power struggle.
2. You teach the child to anticipate fairness in future negotiations.

Define the Issue

Once you get beyond arguing from position, the next step in negotiation is to define the issue. Let's say your child wants to go to another child's house for a party. Your immediate concerns might revolve around a number of issues. Fundamental to all, almost unquestionably, is safety. Will there be parental supervision at the other child's house? Will there be any alcoholic beverages or drugs present? Your child may see the issue as overcontrolling on your part. How the issue is defined is important to resolving the problem.

If the issue is concern for safety, then as a parent, you will have to err on the side of putting safety above all else. If your child insists that what he wants is safe or low-risk, ask for an explanation as to how safety has been considered and what safeguards have been put in place. At this point, you may be charged with the question "Don't you trust me?" Trust is not the issue, safety is—don't be taken off track. You must reassert the issue. It is not about trust. It is about safety.

Focus on your child's interests. Who is going to be at the party? Why does your child want to go to this party? How did he get invited? Which of his friends are going to be there? In short, ask all sorts of relevant questions that children do not usually want to answer. Take your time with the questions and answers. You want your child to understand the importance of thinking things through. Model that approach. If your child insists that you are asking too many questions, politely remind him that you are thinking the issue through and that you would like him to do the same thing.

Repeat Back What You Hear and Think

This is where thinking aloud becomes crucial. Listen to your child and repeat back what you hear while being careful to present his position as fairly as possible. "What I hear you saying is" should be the starting point. If you are able to present what you hear fairly, you take away the possible interpretation that you don't understand what he wants. By repeating back what you hear more clearly and balanced than the child has presented his position, you disarm the child. If you can repeat what you have heard well, the child feels understood even if you don't agree. How can a child be angry in the face of understanding?

Remember, *understanding* the child's point of view is not the same thing as *agreeing* with the child's point of view. The value of thinking out loud—after active listening—allows the parent to state both points of view at the same time. As you read on, you will see that many of the principles expressed by Fisher and Ury dovetail very well with books on negotiation in the adult business world. The principles are the same. In the adult world of negotiation, the need to come to agreement and the rules to do so must be spelled out in a clear and straightforward fashion.

Define Shared Interests

Your child wants to enjoy life and you want that for him. How can this be done safely? Let's continue with two examples of potential conflict—when to begin summer reading and a child wanting to go to a party. Just as parents want their children to be safe, parents want their children to develop good executive functioning and work habits.

The parent wants the child to start summer reading sooner rather than later. The child is tired of school and wants to take some time off before he begins summer reading. If the parent were to present only the parental point of view, it would be expected that the child would respond with the opposite point of view and an argument would follow. Instead, the parent says, "Let me think out loud about this." The parent proceeds to outline two or more possible solutions.

"It's true that you just finished school and I can understand why you would want to take some time off before you begin your summer reading. On the other hand, these things tend to get away from someone if they are not started sooner rather than later. Let me just think this through for moment. If we do not agree with the starting time for summer reading, this could get away from both of us and create a real problem. So, while I can agree to let you postpone the start of your summer reading for a few days, I need to hear a realistic date that will allow you to get your reading done comfortably."

By using this positive strategy, the parent verifies for the child an understanding for his need to take a break from school and the reluctance to get started. On the other hand, the parent is still insisting—albeit in a gentle way—the work must be started soon. The child is being engaged in a positive emotional and caring way.

Outline Possible Choices

Your child wants to go to a party. You have concerns about safety. Questions such as what your child will do if alcohol or drugs are introduced at the party are very appropriate and should get a thoughtful response. Will he contact you or a responsible adult if some other child at the party gets out of line? How does he plan on getting home? Will he call you for a ride or accept a ride from someone at the party? What will he do if he feels pressured to do something he knows you would not approve of? Will he give you the phone number of the responsible parent who is hosting the party? What assurances can your child give you to address these issues? You are asking your child to think of alternatives to respond to your concerns about safety. What you want to hear is that your child is taking safety seriously and not brushing aside your concerns.

In all of these questions, and all of the answers—you are looking for a responsible child—a child you can trust to do the right thing. If your child cannot or will not negotiate, the party may be missed.

Agree on Objective Criteria

Define outcomes and set a time schedule. Also as part of the negotiation, you want the right to review with your child later as to what happened at the party. Who was there? How did the children behave? Did the hosting parents make their presence felt?

Think Out Loud

Let's look at another example. To understand how thinking out loud works, let's consider a common example of something that typically becomes controversial. At some point in the relationship between parent and child, the inevitable clash arises over the matter of the child cleaning his room.

Instead of the usual lecture and resulting fight after your child is told to clean the room, think out loud. Begin by saying something like, "You have told me how you want to go out this weekend with your friends and I have no problem with that as long as you clean your room. I could order you to do it right now or I could let you pick the time as long as it is done an hour before dinner tonight. I think I'll let you pick the time. Just let me know when it's done so I will have time to inspect your work. When would you like to begin?"

What have you accomplished by thinking out loud? The parent started with the conclusion by outlining the reward to be attained and defining two possible alternatives. By doing this, the parent has cut short any discussion about *if* the room is to be cleaned and is using a technique familiar in business—the assumptive closing. (We are going to get this done. We are negotiating when it will be done.) We are not talking about whether the room is to be cleaned; we know the answer to that. We are trying to establish a starting time as well as a finishing time. Thinking out loud allows the speaker to present both sides—and many sides—of a dilemma or situation without appearing to take a position at the outset. There always has to be the presumption that following a parental directive is the right and smart thing to do and you have the strong belief that your child will understand this and do what is right.

Share a Summer Reading with Your Child

Suppose a parent were to pick up some of the books on the child's summer reading list and read it at the same time as the child, thus reinforcing the impetus to complete the assignment. It is also a great opportunity for the parent to discuss a book and examine what values are being taught in a less directive way than the usual style of communication they might have.

Let's take another look at a classic book that became a movie. *To Kill a Mockingbird,* is a story told primarily through the eyes of two small children, Jem and Scout. After reading the book, questions can be raised and asked directly of the reader. An example of some questions:

1. The two children have a preconceived idea about the character of Boo Radley. What was their preconceived idea? Should people rush to judgment or should they learn more before making a judgment?

2. With regard to the character of Atticus Finch:

   What kind of courage did it take for Atticus to do the right thing?

   What would've happened if Atticus did not do what he did?

Chapter 3 Questions

Am I thinking out loud and defining choices?

Am I looking for books and movies I can share with my child?

Chapter 4

HOW BAD ARE THINGS?

If you are reading this, chances are you're having some kind of problem with your child and you are asking yourself a variation of the question "How did things go wrong and what can I do to change it?"

Whenever I hear parents wondering how things had gone wrong, I think of Marlon Brando as Don Corleone in *The Godfather* when he sat down with a somewhat bewildered look on his face to ask the question of the other members of the five families, "How did it all come to this?" Sometimes when things go wrong, it can seem like they are spinning out of control rapidly. People invariably wonder, when did this all begin or what can I do about it?

That's the question that parents most frequently ask themselves. After all, you have been a good parent. Well, that's at least part of the problem—you may have been too good, too generous. You gave things to your children because you wanted your children to have advantages you perhaps didn't have. Giving things away for nothing, or worse yet, rewarding bad behavior can create problems.

If you give things and privileges away for nothing—guess what? The privileges that you give away for nothing are worth just that—nothing. It took some time as well as lack of awareness on your part to get into this fix and it is going to take a good deal of time and effort to get out of it. After all, the kids are not going to want to change—can you blame them? Why would they want to do away with Santa Claus when they are the beneficiaries of his giveaways? You tell yourself, you have been a good parent; you love your children and have always tried to do what is best for them—even if they disagree at times about that last part.

Now, you have to ask yourself the next question, "How can I get my child to change?" The problem here is one of motivation. The child who's been rewarded for doing nothing or for doing something wrong is not going to want to change. A better question to ask might be: "Can I motivate my child to change and if so, how?" To answer this question, let's take a look at behavioral psychology.

Motivate Your Child

There is an anecdotal story told about B. F. Skinner, a famous behavioral psychologist, on the subject of motivation. Dr. Skinner was being observed while working with his usual subjects, white rats. In this case, he was working with rats swimming in a pool and measuring the speed of the rats to reach the reinforcer, which was food. He was doing this under various conditions that he could regulate such as the temperature of the water.

The temperature of the water was systematically lowered on each successive trial and what Dr. Skinner found was that as the water got colder, the rats swam faster. Now, it should be remembered that Dr. Skinner dealt solely with stimulus and response with no intervening variables such as feelings. With that in mind, the stage was set for a somewhat seemingly unusual exchange between the observer and Dr. Skinner. When asked if the rats swam faster because they wanted to get out of the cold water, Dr. Skinner, replied "I do not know about that but at lower temperatures they swim faster."

What does Dr. Skinner's finding have to do with your kids? As parents, we know we cannot always give the child the motivation (that's an internal variable) to do anything. However, we can, and sometimes should, do something within the home environment to make the water colder or warmer depending on the circumstances. As it has been incorporated into the mainstream of cognitive behavior therapy, Dr. Skinner's work with rats has long since been developed and modified by subsequent theories.

Using the principles of cognitive behavior therapy requires a good deal of preparation and education. For parents already facing multiple tasks, it means additional work and learning a few behavioral principles. You may wonder if all the effort is worth it? The answer is clearly yes. When the principles of behavior and negotiation are applied correctly, the up-front investment of time and energy is repaid in long-term dividends to the parent and child alike.

In addition, learning good negotiation skills is crucial to adapting in the world. Pushing negative thoughts out of one's head and staying focused on a goal will carry over into almost everything one does in life. Learning and applying good behavioral principles may not be easy. It may be difficult at times and you may make mistakes. You cannot be fixated on doing everything perfectly at the beginning. Do not get overly concerned about making a few mistakes as you go forward. Everything takes practice.

Mistakes: They're Going to Happen!
There are always going to be times when you or your child is on the edge of being out of control and saying or doing something regretful. You will lose control, as will your child. You need to regain control as soon as possible to prevent further damage. How do you get the need for control across? Let's examine the use of metaphor and a movie.

When it comes to the topic of what to do with mistakes, take a look at the way skiing is taught. What do you think of—gliding effortlessly down a mountain or experiencing the panic of being out of control? If you have ever taken a skiing lesson, you remember the first thing taught is how to fall down. A class of beginners is directed to just sit back on their skis and fall backward. Once the beginners are safely on the ground, they are taught the second step—how to stand up. On the slopes, they are taught, "If you're going too fast and feel out of control, simply sit back on your skis. It's the safest way to fall and not get hurt."

The art of teaching skiing is taught differently in the 1985 film *Better Off Dead*. Someone offers skiing advice to Lane Meyer (John Cusack), who is standing at the top of a mountain. The person giving the advice to Lane points down a very steep slope on the mountain and offers no advice other than to say, "Go that way, really fast and if something is in your way—turn." Going straight down a mountain out of control is not a good idea; it's also not a good idea to do anything else in an out-of-control way. Our hero in the movie does get down the mountain but in an out-of-control tumble. While the audience may enjoy Lane Meyer's tumble, it is not something a sensible person would try without some practice first!

The point to practicing is to feel and be in control as a sensible approach to handling situations. However, despite how much you practice, you will find yourself with control issues. You will make mistakes, but mistakes are not the real problem. Learning how not to give up and to recover is the challenge. *The only mistake that cannot be recovered is the one you believe you cannot repair.* You will make many mistakes before you become competent and you will make them after you become competent. So, what are you to do when you make a mistake? Be prepared to metaphorically fall back on your skis. Stop—do not make things worse by going forward.

What does this have to do with your kids? When you get into a struggle with your child, you will sometimes become upset—maybe even very upset. You may feel out of control at times and feel you're going too fast down a slippery slope. You cannot put on the brakes because skis have no brakes. When you are going too fast—when you're starting to feel out of control—keep the metaphor of skiing in mind and remember to sit back and down. Get over the need for immediate results. Time is on your side.

Get Control Over *You*

The first thing you will have to accomplish is to learn how to be in control of yourself. If you're hoping to influence your children in positive ways for the future, the best thing you can do is give them a role model to follow in how to handle situations and other people. You may not be able to change anyone else but you can certainly change you. And here is the important part: If you change you, others will change. Proceed with the idea in mind that the only person you can really change is you. If you tell someone else to change or, even worse, order them to change, it is likely you will not achieve your goal. Others will disagree with you, argue with you, and most likely not change. However, if you change yourself and tell the other person what you will and will not reward with regard to that person's behavior, you will have created an atmosphere in which change can occur.

Keep the choices you give your child simple and avoid arguing. Arguing is not negotiation. It is almost a principle: No one will change until you successfully make changes to yourself. *Once you make changes to yourself, you will find that everyone else in your life will change.*

Parents will have a full range of emotions in dealing with their children. They will be happy for them, proud of them, upset with them, and angry with them. Parents will experience the full feelings of the gamut. You can't control how you feel but you can control how you act on your feelings. You must learn to express feelings in words but refrain from acting out your feelings in behavior. Children—not adults—act out on feelings.

Can You Control Your Feelings?

You really have no control over your feelings. You are going to feel what you feel in response to people and situations. You cannot control how you feel; however, you do and should have control over how you choose to express those feelings. Telling a child you are upset with his behavior and asking for change is much more effective—and definitely a good deal safer—than an angry rant. When your children were younger, you may have perceived yourself as being more in control. They could be picked up, moved around and told to do things as you directed. There may have been some upset and tears but muscle carried the day. You got what you asked for—compliance. Even if your child managed to mount a full-scale rebellion, it was usually short-lived.

As a child gets a little older and begins to defy the parent with a "No," the parent tends to raise his or her voice and responds with anger, "How dare you refuse to do what I tell you to do!" As time passes, your child perhaps having adjusted to your raised voice, no longer responds the same way. Children begin to act out with defiant refusals or temper tantrums—or even worse with protracted rebellions.

The reality is should this happen, you're going to get upset with your child. Act smart and do not act out on your feelings either with bad behavior or an angry rant. It is one thing to say, "I'm angry that you did…(whatever the behavior)." It is quite another to respond with anger. Shouting at your child only throws fuel on the fire. If you respond with angry rants, think of the behavior you are now modeling. You are giving your child a negative demonstration of how he should deal with feelings, and it will come back to haunt you.

You Will Feel Frustration

When you are beginning this process, you will experience a certain amount of frustration—perhaps a great deal of frustration. Frustration, as the psychology textbooks tell us, is half a word—the rest of the word is "aggression." It is what is commonly called the Frustration-Aggression hypothesis. Frustration is experienced when a seemingly inconvenient or insurmountable obstacle is placed in front of a goal that you believed you were just about to reach. At the last second, the goal is snatched away, leaving you frustrated. Frustration is something we all experience.

As an example of frustration, imagine going to a soda machine on a hot day. You are hot and thirsty for a cold drink. You put money in the machine and after you push the button no beverage comes out. You try a few other buttons with the same result. Then you hit the coin return. You are further frustrated because the machine keeps the change!

What's a person to do? How many times have you seen someone in the workplace smack the soda machine? That person is acting out the experienced frustration. Will hitting the machine do anything? No. Still, there's something primal about the whole thing, maybe a feeling that you got back at the machine!

The same kind of thing happens with interactions between people. We become frustrated and want to strike out. Now ask yourself the question—do you want to be a primal person or a thinking person? There is another way; there is always another way.

Meta-communication Is a Needed Tool: Reason, Don't Rant

Instead of an angry rant, suppose you were to employ some form of meta-communication. Meta-communication is simply a communication about a communication. You may not be familiar with the specific term *meta-communication* but you have used it yourself many times in the course of dealing with others. Teachers and parents use meta-communication frequently. You are using meta-communication whenever you say to someone, "Pay attention," or "I need you to listen to what I'm saying." You have not said anything other than just letting someone know that you are going to say something you think is important.

An Example of Meta-communication and Thinking Out Loud

Suppose you were to say, "Let me think out loud about this. I'm upset with your failure to keep your word. You promised to have your room cleaned by now but you obviously have not done that. We need to take a look at what our options are. Now, the next thing I tell you is very important. I want you to listen carefully."

You really haven't said anything of importance yet concerning what you're going to do. You're just telling your child that the next thing you say is the important thing (meta-communication). When you have your child's attention, you can continue. "I could get angry, raise my voice, and act out on my anger, but I do not want to do that. I do not think you want that, either. So if you're willing to listen, we'll reason this out together. We will figure out how you can earn what you want without your life being disrupted and I will not have to raise my voice. So, do I have your attention? Is this a good time for you? If it is not, we can talk later."

Faced with an angry parent as opposed to a parent with whom your child can reason, the likelihood of arriving at a mutually agreeable solution increases. Does it take control to do this when you're upset? Absolutely it does; however, the rewards both in the present and down the road are well worth it. Despite this, you will make mistakes. And when you do, be ready to offer an apology. Remember, you are trying to train your child to respond appropriately to a mistake.

It's Important to Learn How to Apologize

Okay, let's say you have already raised your voice and yelled. Back to the skiing example—you got out of control and forgot to fall down. How do you walk that back? Something to keep in mind—and it bears repeating—is that you will make mistakes, many of them. It's important for you to learn how to apologize to your child not only to convey a sense of responsibility and regret for an action; but also, to begin to model for your child how he should respond when making a mistake. An apology will be required. You can say, "I'm sorry I raised my voice. Let's start over again."

The really crucial part about an apology is not to simply say, "I'm sorry." The important part of an apology is to do things differently in the future—to do things in a better way and to make amends for negative behavior. An apology based on behavior says, "I made a mistake, I take responsibility for it and to show you I mean that I'm sorry, I'm going to show you by my behavior that I can act differently." (More about an apology in a later chapter.)

Chapter 4 Questions

Am I giving rewards away for nothing or rewarding bad behavior?

Am I admitting and correcting myself when I make a mistake?

Am I slowing things down when voices are being raised?

Am I able to act intelligently even when getting upset?

Chapter 5

BUILDING POSITIVE CHANGES BEGINS WITH AWARENESS OF SELF AND OTHERS: AWARENESS IS NOT AS SIMPLE AS IT MIGHT FIRST SEEM

How often does your work schedule affect the amount of quality time you have to spend with your child and how does it affect the consistency of your response to your child's behavior? It seems obvious that the busier you are, the less time you have available to deal with your children's issues as they arise. We live in a world of work. We manage schedules that often leave us tired at the end of the day and therefore more prone to overlooking or avoiding issues at home. Children live in a world of texting and video games and as such, they are often living in a world outside of our awareness. When parents are tired or feeling overwhelmed, this separation becomes greater, increasing the chances you'll not notice when something is amiss. There is a tendency toward not taking action and the increased tendency to ignore bad behavior. You tell yourself you will deal with a problem later. Consequently, your child winds up sitting with a cell phone in hand texting with friends—or in front of the TV or the game box—as you try to unwind in peace and quiet.

If you think about it, you would probably agree that you have not noticed something going wrong until a message comes from the school about your child missing homework assignments. Occasionally, you may have been guilty of ignoring noncooperative or even bad behavior. While *ignoring* bad behavior is not as bad as *rewarding* bad behavior, your lack of intervention can have important consequences. Maybe your mind was preoccupied and in your distracted mode you gave something away simply without realizing it—a reward like TV or game box time—thinking of it as merely a means to pacify your child. Maybe you have even rewarded your child for noncooperative behavior despite the fact that you know it is not a good idea to set a pattern of rewards in this situation. Maybe you just did it to be a nice parent and make your child happy. Or maybe you were in a rush and wanted to move on and avoid having to deal with a situation that came at the *wrong* time—as though there is ever a *right* time.

Do We Really Think About What Is Going On?

Let us revisit neuroscience for some possible answers as to why we sometimes fail to take notice of action when in a clearer moment, we realize we would have noticed and taken corrective measures. Perhaps we are not as in charge as much as we would like to imagine, for reasons other than our conscious awareness.

Neuroscience has increasingly been discovering that we are not the thinking people we have been assumed to be. According to cognitive neuroscience research, we are conscious of only a small part of what we do on a daily basis. Numerous cognitive neuroscientists have conducted studies that have revealed that only 5 percent of our cognitive activities are conscious whereas the remaining 95 percent is generated in a non-conscious manner. Timothy Wilson has referred to this phenomenon as the "adaptive unconscious" in his book *Strangers To Ourselves*. Dr. Wilson describes the adaptive unconscious as "mental processes that are more inaccessible to consciousness but influences judgments, feelings and behaviors." He contends that the things that we do on a daily basis are done on automatic pilot, a concept later popularized by Malcolm Gladwell in his book *Blink: Thinking Without Thinking.*

Do we really know ourselves? Do other people see us as we see ourselves? Neuroscientist Heidi Grant Halvorson, author of *You Are (Probably) Wrong About You,* points out that our own perception of our personality traits compare with the impressions of other people who know us well at a correlation rate of .40 percent. In other words, how you see yourself and how other people see you are only partially one and the same. Who's right? Who knows best? Well, the research suggests that other people's assessment of your personality predicts your behavior, on average, better than your assessment does.

What Does This Mean and How Does It Affect Us?

Years ago, while I was a senior in high school, we were presented with a series of workshops designed to help us make career choices. People in various fields, many of whom were doing exciting things, conducted the workshops. There were doctors, lawyers and a series of people involved in the sciences and commercial business. One day we had a workshop given by a businessman from a supermarket chain. At the start of the lecture, most of us were not very interested in what this man had to say because we were predominantly engrossed in the more exciting careers involving science and discovery.

The speaker began his talk by saying, "I know a great deal about all of you. See, you think I'm in the supermarket business—well, I'm really in the people business." This immediately captured my attention as I wondered what it was he thought he knew. The speaker commented that we were all creatures of habit. He went on to explain that because we were all from a specific part of the city, he knew pretty much what we had for dinner each week. We associated with the same friends. We went to the same kinds of movies, went in and out of the same doors. If we ate popcorn, we ordered popcorn at the movies. He went on to explain that our parents were equally as predictable. People generally shopped the same day of the week, week after week. The supermarket could calculate how many turkeys to order in preparation for Thanksgiving because all they had to do was look to see how many turkeys were sold the previous year. As a high school senior, I was astounded to think that I was already a creature of habit and that all of us, without realizing it, were so obviously predictable. We were doing things in our everyday life—on automatic pilot—without consciously thinking about it.

The adaptive unconscious is at work throughout the day. Because we have so much to do each day, our brain utilizes the adaptive unconscious and works at simplifying the choices we have to make in order to make us more efficient. But, as Wilson points out, efficiency and speed come at a cost, as "the adaptive unconscious can choose a different goal from the one we might have chosen had we gone about it consciously."

The brain works to create working patterns. While we are capable of problem solving, for the most part we rely upon previous consistent patterns of behavior. We refer to these consistent patterns of behavior as habits. The adaptive unconscious makes it possible for us to get up in the morning, dress, eat, and drive to work, all with a minimum of thought. If we had to stop and think about what we would wear, what we would have for breakfast every morning, or what route we would take to get to work, we would probably be running late most days. The adaptive unconscious is the brain's autopilot.

When you were not aware and did not really think about a specific incident involving your child—in the context of a pattern of a series of behaviors—you may well have been on autopilot. While being on autopilot makes us more efficient because we do not have to think through every step, it can come at a cost when things go wrong. When we cannot utilize the unconscious self, we lose efficiency and can easily become stuck as to what to do. Our minds have no unconscious way to handle new and novel situations and no practiced ways to handle the situation in which we find ourselves. Now, we must consciously think about what to do.

Obviously the first step in getting control is becoming aware of what is happening. Stop giving things away for nothing. You make a situation—any situation—worse when you give things away for nothing. Actually the problem is sometimes worse than just giving things away for nothing. It has longer-term consequences.

When you are exhausted, there is a tendency toward giving up and caving in to bad behavior just so you can get some peace of mind. It is difficult to stay strong when you are tired—but think of the consequences if you do not. If you give up and relent when things get tough, you are teaching your child to fight on until you wear out. You are actually encouraging your child and rewarding her for being obstinate.

Are You Giving Things Away for Nothing? "Reward Bad Behavior? I Do Not Do That!"

Years ago while consulting at a high school, I was approached by a respected teacher who was also a department head. She explained that since the death of her husband, she was feeling overwhelmed at home and needed help to deal with her three children. I was frankly surprised to hear what she was saying because she possessed such an aura of confidence and competency at school. It seemed incredible to me that such a self-assured person in the workplace could be having problems at home dealing with school-age children. My colleague explained that since the death of her husband, things were getting worse. She would come home from school and do the essentials: make dinner, prepare her lesson for the next day, and check to make sure her children did their homework. Then, she would try to shut her world out by putting on headphones and listening to music while the children did almost whatever they pleased. Not surprisingly, ignoring bad behavior was not the answer. What my colleague needed were the tools to deal with problems. Once these tools were put in place, the discord at home diminished greatly and she was able to enjoy her children again.

Developing Plan B Is the Upside to the Downside of Loss of Efficiency

Because habit patterns can be so firmly established, you may be at a loss to handle something outside the usual. You may not have a Plan B to activate. You become angry and frustrated. You tell yourself you do not have the strength or energy to keep harping on your child and that it's easier to do things yourself. You tell yourself, "I have to pick my battles and this does not seem that important." When this happens, you are actually rewarding uncooperative behavior.

You must do the right thing even if you are tired—especially when you are tired. You must overcome the tendency to say to yourself, "I cannot do this otherwise I will be fighting about every little thing." Well, it will seem like that in the beginning and it may get worse before it gets better.

Remember, your child is creating his own habit pattern that, once established, will either make his life and yours a good deal better or worse. If your child responds in outrage at being denied something and you have no Plan B, you may well display outrage of your own. You have placed yourself in the unenviable position of your child acting out maniac behavior while you are at a loss as to how to respond. When your child is rebelling or acting like a maniac, this is the time for thinking through a response to your child. As the parent, you do not want to lose it and join in the maniac behavior—because if you do, you'll be teaching the wrong thing and become a maniac yourself. This brings us to a principle: No matter what the provocation, do not let yourself turn into a maniac.

When things go wrong, you're likely to feel the strong need to do something about it right away. You may raise your voice. You may lecture and depending upon the response your lecture receives, you will either calm down or become more upset.

Suppose you have just lectured your child for some objectionable behavior. Your child listens passively to the lecture and soon afterward, asks for a ride to the mall. What do you do now? You delivered your lecture and you think your child has heard you. He was looking at you, but was he listening? You cannot let your child walk to the mall, so you give your child a ride without being sure he will demonstrate more desirable behavior in the future. Look at it from the child's point of view: I fight with my parent, listen to a lecture and get away with it by getting a ride to the mall. Guess what? You just rewarded your child for fighting with you!

Certainly, you have some perfectly good reason for allowing your child to go to the mall; such as you want to have distance from the child. However, if the ride comes on the heels of the fight with no good behavior in between, you are running a free taxi service. You are rewarding the behavior you do not want. Forget about the fiery lecture you think you may have delivered; your behavior is more definitive than the lecture. More important, your child is not buying your lecture. Lectures reward passivity because children do not have to respond, they only have to listen dutifully until their parents wear themselves out and stop talking. As a parent, ask yourself, "Is my child listening?" More important, ask yourself, "Does my child agree?" As a rule, if you lecture, you lose.

Let's take a look at another example. Suppose your child has not done homework, straightened up the room, made the bed, or done any other expected household chore. You insist that some—maybe even just one—of the tasks be done before he can go out. Your child argues with you and you agree that he can go out and clean up the room upon his return. You have succumbed to the "I'll do it later" plea. You did it again! You were taken unaware and had no Plan B ready for action. Perhaps you just saw your child's behavior as a single act and not the start of a pattern of behavior. Maybe you just did not know how to respond. This is why it is so important to have a Plan B.

What Are the Long-Term Dangers of Overlooking Non-responsible Behavior?

As a parent, you should want to reward competency and responsibility in your children. If you reward incompetency and irresponsibility, it stands to reason you will keep getting ineffectual behavior.

You may ask yourself, "What would happen if I were to model the behavior I want from my child?" Simply modeling the behavior you want may not be enough and, in fact, it may produce the opposite effect. You have probably noticed in the workplace that employees who are really confident often get a greater workload than those who are not as competent (or who at least act as though they are not as competent). Frequently, those who do less and who cannot be counted upon are often *rewarded* with less responsibility—as the responsible people take on increasing responsibilities.

This same kind of modeling consequence can happen at home. The more competent that you are and the more work that you do for everyone else, the less the child has to do. Do things get better for you? Does everyone love you more and want to do more for you? Possibly. However, doing more for your children does not necessarily translate into gaining appreciation or greater productivity from your child. You are unconsciously expecting some form of reciprocation in return. After all, you get everyone up, make breakfast, etc., all with a smile. Slowly at first, you may begin to feel unappreciated. If you are a kind and generous parent and try to demonstrate the right thing to do—you are possibly getting ready to turn into a maniac yourself if your behavior is seldom imitated.

What's Wrong with the "Nice Guy" Approach?

You want to be the nice guy. Okay, maybe being the nice guy works for a few people. But very few people have no trouble with always being the nice guy, doing things for others without getting anything (or very little in return) and without seemingly ever voicing displeasure at what others do. However, beneath the nice-guy exterior there is often a maniac lying in wait—waiting to emerge after the inevitable burnout.

No one is more frightening than a nice guy who is about to lose it. The nice guy is someone who lets things build up inside without expressing the rising hurt and anger until the moment when it cannot be held back any longer—"I've had enough!" When feelings of frustration, hurt and anger take over, the nice guy lets someone have it for a whole long list of offenses. No one can predict when the nice guy is going to lose it, but the nice guy will eventually lose it. And, when the nice guy does lose it—it will not be pretty.

You May Not Be Able to Spot That You Are About to "Lose It"
People who go around doing things for others without asking for anything in return, not surprisingly, usually get nothing, or next to nothing, in return. That sounds bad enough but it's actually worse than that. Because when someone goes around spoiling others into thinking that they are entitled to be treated well without having to show any effort in return—a dangerous paradigm is set in place. What is the child actually learning from being the recipient of rewards without earning them? Much has been written about the time we live in…often referred to as the age of the "helicopter parent." The parent is seen as a hovering helicopter ready to sweep into action to rescue the child from having to assume responsibility. Just as the human mind, a helicopter can operate on autopilot.

You do so much while so little has been given in return. The potential explosion comes when the parent asks the child to do something seemingly simple and expected (clean your room, do your homework, turn in missing school assignments). The child who is indulged may well have developed a pattern of ignoring his parent and react negatively to any demand on his time. What message is the child receiving from being the recipient of rewards unearned? Answer: "I have the right to be indulged. You taught me, you trained me, and I like it this way." Since you do so much and ask for so little, Mr. or Ms. Nice Guy, prepare to become a maniac.

Before You Lose It, Give Yourself a Break

You need to start paying attention to what you are rewarding. Are you rewarding positive behaviors or negative behaviors? If you do not react and object to negative behavior, you're probably rewarding it. If you are rewarding negative behavior—the child who simply seems to do nothing—it's no wonder you're not getting any cooperation. You have unknowingly put yourself on the road to becoming a maniac. If turning this behavior around seems like a daunting task, you may well be a worn-out parent. Being worn out does not mean you will *not* turn into a maniac. You just need to be pushed a little further than many other parents.

In the course of my practice, I have met many competent adults who are very successful in their respective fields whether it is in medicine, business or law. However, despite their confidence and competence in their chosen careers, their children are winning virtually every battle at home. Why is this? Are some parents under the mistaken idea that they deserve to relax when they get home?

If you want change in your children's behavior, you must begin to talk and act differently. You will need some tools to work with. You will need a Plan B. First, you will need to practice your responses consciously so Plan B becomes part of your new adaptive unconscious. Your Plan B should always include the 3 Strategies Approach: Ask questions, tell stories, and think out loud.

Chapter 5 Questions

Am I rewarding behavior I do not want?

Am I able to recognize when I'm "losing" it?

Am I able to step back when I realize I'm losing it?

Chapter 6

A MOVING TARGET: THE CHILD KEEPS CHANGING

If much of what we do is based on unconscious habit patterns, then it is likely that how we handle a current situation will be similar to the way we handled comparable situations in the past. Under similar conditions, we are likely to respond on autopilot. However, because your child is growing and changing, things may look similar but be quite different. What worked yesterday may not work today.

As your child grows, places or settings will change to produce different sets of circumstances. Dealing with your child at home may be quite different from dealing with him in a public environment. As an example, your child's behavior is likely to be different with his peers or when he is in school. All the while, your child is learning his own habit patterns of responses.

You Need to Learn New Skills to Handle New Situations: Why?
You may ask yourself: Why do I need to learn new skills? The answer lies in the fact that you are trying to hit a moving target. The child you are dealing with today is different from the one you dealt with yesterday. The situations you encounter change as your child grows and adapts to the way you handled matters in the past. Is your child getting smarter to your ways of dealing with him? You have options: You can wait until there is a problem

and be reactive, or you can be proactive by anticipating situations in practiced ways to handle potential problems before they occur.

Why Won't My Child Just Follow Orders?
You may look back wistfully to an earlier time when you gave an order and it was obeyed. And if it was not obeyed, you could force your will on the child. Now, faced with a growing child, an order is likely to draw a "Why?" or "Why not?" before there is any sign of compliance. You may find you are caught in a back-and-forth question-and-answer session with your child—and it is he who is asking all the questions!

Inevitably, out of frustration, you found yourself saying something like, "Because I said so, that's why." The rebellion against your authority, which began with a simple "Why?" is a question that can't be answered without drawing another series of "why" questions. In the rebellion, you are faced with a child who now sounds suspiciously like an attorney arguing with what he may call your repressive and out-of-touch point of view. Sometimes parents may feel like they are dealing with the proverbial jail-house lawyer.

As your child matures, he is on a course to acquire freedom; as a parent, you may be seen either as an obstacle to that destination or someone who helps provide the tools to succeed in life. How best to help your child grow into a responsible adult is the issue.

An Argument in the Store
Practically everyone has had the experience of walking into a store as a conflict is taking place between the storeowner and an irate customer. If you're like me, you watched carefully, trying to gauge how explosive the argument might become, as you got ready to run for the door. Regardless of what is being said, one thing you quickly became aware of was that one person was winning and one was losing. Without listening to the exact words that

are exchanged, it takes the average person only seconds to make an easy deduction—the person who is shouting is losing. The person shouting is out-of-control. We instinctively move away from the shouting maniac.

The storeowner is at an immediate disadvantage. After all, the customer is always *right*—at least, that is the popular cultural narrative. Other customers watching may well tend to identify with a fellow customer. The storeowner, in the hot seat, is out-numbered and being observed appraisingly. He does not want to seem unreasonable and risk scaring potential customers away and so he must be on his best professional behavior. Conversely, the customer may have no such worries about being judged and may be intent on having his way regardless of what others may think.

If the storeowner gives in, he may lose money. If he does not give in and maintains his position, he may well lose customers. The storeowner is in the classic double bind situation—damned if he does and damned if he does not. The one thing the storeowner must do is stay in control—not lose it like the customer.

What Is a Double Bind? The Double Bind Is the Classic "No-Win"– Lose-Lose Situation!

Simply stated, the double bind is a situation in which someone cannot either do, or not do, an action in response to either of two options without being wrong. There are perhaps better portrayals of the double bind but none funnier than the one found in the classic movie *Catch-22*. In one scene, a military bombardier, Captain Yossarian (Alan Arkin), is pleading with the doctor to ground him so he will not have to fly dangerous missions over Germany. He says, "I don't want to fly anymore, it's dangerous." The captain continues and asks, "Can you ground someone who is crazy?" The doctor responds, "Yes, it's a rule, I have to ground anyone who is crazy…but they have to ask me." The catch, as the doctor explains, is that: "Anyone who wants to get out of combat isn't really crazy so I can't ground him." Captain Yossarian responds, "Let me see if I've got this straight. To be grounded, I have got to be crazy and I must be crazy to keep flying. But, if I ask to be grounded, I'm not crazy anymore and I have to keep flying."

In a military situation, an officer orders a private to stand at attention. The officer asks the soldier, "Why were the windows in the barracks left open last night?" The soldier begins to answer but is quickly cut off by the officer who says, "You're at attention. No excuses!" The soldier immediately stops talking and the officer continues, "I gave you a direct order. I ordered you to tell me why the windows were left open last night?" The soldier tries to respond. Again, he is told by the officer to stand at attention and make no excuses. We have a double bind. The soldier cannot obey one order without disobeying the other order and is denied the opportunity to comment on the injustice of the situation.

We can draw from the movie *Full Metal Jacket* another example of the double bind. In the film, the marine called Private Joker is asked by the senior drill instructor if he believes in the Virgin Mary. When the private responds, "Sir, negative, sir." The senior drill instructor slaps the private and demands that he reverse his answer and affirm his belief in the Virgin Mary. Once again, the private responds, "Sir, negative, sir." There is another slap by the drill instructor, as he demands a different answer from the private.

The private is now stuck. If he reverses his answer, he will be seen as doing so because he does not want to be struck again. The private loses because his reversal will be seen as cowardly and unacceptable behavior as a marine. If the private does not reverse his position, he will likely continue to be struck. This option is also unacceptable and not very smart.

How to Negotiate Your Way Out of the Double Bind
The private finds a way out of the situation by exposing the double bind while saying, "Sir, the private believes that the senior drill instructor will beat him harder if he reverses his decision, sir." The private is "stepping outside the situation" by thinking

out loud and pointing out the absurdity of the situation. It is now the senior drill who is stuck. If the drill instructor continues the demand for a reversal and slaps the private, it is the drill instructor that has placed himself in a double bind. What does the drill instructor do? The drill instructor stops slapping the private and places him in charge of the squad because he "...has got guts."

It is by staying in control and pointing out the lose-lose situation that we see our way out of the double bind. The senior drill instructor was out of control and the private was in control because he retained his reason in the face of an intense confrontation.

How Does the Double Bind Relate to an Interaction Between Parent and Child?

Could you get caught in a situation where others are watching a confrontation between you and your child? Not so long ago, a woman came to my office to relate a story that occurred when she went shopping with her daughter. Once inside the mall, the daughter asked her mother to buy her an expensive pair of boots. The mother thought the boots were overpriced and not needed. Within seconds, the request turned into a demand with the twelve-year-old raising her voice loudly. The mother was embarrassed as she noticed the attention the incident was attracting. An argument ensued with the mother declaring the shopping trip was over and that her daughter should get in the car because they were going home. The argument escalated as the daughter refused to leave the store. Mom was stuck. She did not want to give in by purchasing the item while at the same time not knowing how to get her child to go with her to the car. The mother felt mortified to be humiliated in public. Mom became a victim of a double bind. Feeling frustrated and self-conscious, Mom gave in and bought the boots. Her question for the therapy session was—what could she do differently to prevent similar situations from happening in the future? (I'll circle back to handling difficult circumstances like this later.)

What to Do?

The first step is to stay in control. Just like the storeowner, if the mother stays under control—and it is the daughter who is raising her voice—it is obvious who has the problem. Sometimes when you are stuck, you are just stuck and you might as well accept it.

As the parent, it all starts with you. Thus, the principle: *Stay in Control*, and certainly do not shout or yell—because if you do, you will sound like an out-of-control maniac. Did you ever look in the Help Wanted section of the newspaper to see if there are job openings for people who are having problems controlling themselves? Don't waste your time. No one is likely to run an ad for "Maniac wanted, short hours, good pay, and great benefits." No, there is no demand for maniacs.

Getting In Control Is a Fundamental Step to Learn

What is the first thing we are all taught to do in a crisis situation? Don't panic! Don't yell! Try to speak in a calm voice when telling others what to do.

What should you do? Getting in control is the basic and most fundamental step in dealing effectively in any situation especially in circumstances involving your child. This means retaining your composure in the knowledge that you will always win—maybe not right now but in the long run—as long as you do not lose it and start yelling back. Despite this knowledge, you probably have to admit that you have raised your voice and yelled at your child. Why not? Sometimes it is necessary to raise your voice to convey emergency information and danger to stop or warn your child when something bad may happen to him. It is not those times that are a problem; it is those other times when you raise your voice and yelled from fatigue or frustration. And, there will be those occasions when you just do not want to take the time and energy to explain the reasoning behind your directions.

It is those other times that put a parent at risk. Your child will take his cue from you—if you shout, the child will shout and/or act out. Now, we all know that so why do we do it? The

answer is easy—we have learned to do it because it works—
sometimes—and that is the problem. When shouting works, you
have been rewarded for doing something the wrong way. You
are like the inveterate gambler who believes he is on a winning
streak because he won a bet. Actually, all that happened was that
you got away with something that you should not have gotten
away with—you got lucky.

Shouting Is a Slippery Slope

When shouting sometimes works we experience great immediate
success. The emphasis is on the word *sometimes*. How many times
have you heard someone say with triumph in his voice, "I gave
him a piece of my mind!" Spurred on by self-perceived success,
the person continues to gain what he wants through intimidation.
The trouble is that your child becomes accustomed to shouting
and begins shouting back. That's right, to continue this approach
you are teaching your child to shout! It's a vicious cycle—you
now must shout back louder! Or, you resort to other methods
of control and ground your child. "You're grounded!" you say
in an angry tone of voice. If your child continues to be defiant,
you increase the punishment. The grounding is extended from
minutes to hours...from days to weeks...any time period that will
make an impression...for the weekend...for the rest of her life!
You are on a slippery slope. The problem with this type of punishment is that it will have a very real, unintended consequence.
Someone will have to be present to enforce the punishment. It
will be *you* and your child.

This brings us to another principle: Never punish yourself
while intending to punish someone else. Are you winning? No,
because you are about to lose freedom. You are putting yourself
in a self-imposed double bind.

How does this work and how have you put yourself in a double bind? Let's go back to the example of grounding your child.
You have a grounded child on your hands who resents you. You
are in big trouble. In order to enforce the grounding, you have

to stay home. You tell yourself, my child deserves the imposed sentence. Then you may think...I don't want to punish myself... but now you think, I said it and I cannot go back on my word and release my child from imprisonment. You are stuck. That doesn't sound very smart.

So if you believe you can't go back on your word because your child will win you are both stuck. What has been gained? Who wins? Answer: Nobody wins! Acting in anger escalates a situation and is a bad approach.

It Is Vital to Be In Control of Yourself

Get control of yourself. You do not need to shout to be quietly intimidating. Let's look at a story of control from a movie. Why do I keep using films to illustrate points? Because films tell stories!

One of the most popular films of the 1990s was *Silence of the Lambs,* which won five Academy Awards. Anthony Hopkins plays the terrifying character of Hannibal Lecter. (Did you know that he was on screen for a total of only twenty-one minutes?) What made Hannibal Lecter so scary? Is it because we know he had the reputation as a killer? Not really, although that probably helped. These days there are many killers in movies but none nearly as scary as Hannibal.

Mr. Hopkins commented that when he read the script, he knew immediately how to play the villain. Mr. Hopkins decided to lose some weight for the role to appear leaner and enhance the image of a man in control of himself. He knew, that to create the image he wanted, everything about Lecter had to be deliberate and measured—in his words and appearance. Mr. Hopkins was so effective in creating the fearsome and calculating character of Hannibal Lecter that it overflowed to off-screen. People moved away from him when he came on the set. No one in the cast or crew would approach or talk to him. In the morning, Mr. Hopkins had to come to the set and make jokes with the crew so people would relax.

Control Gets Attention

I am not suggesting that you try to terrify your children. To project control you need to look like you are under control. Easier said than done, you might say. Suppose you are dealing with your child and you find yourself losing it. Get away and take a break. It is okay to do so—in fact, it is recommended. Just stop and say, "I need to think about this. I'll deal with you later."

Stepping Back Can Be a Positive Use of Anxiety

If you step back, guess what is likely to happen? Your child does not want you to stop. The child wants to get this over with to lessen his anxiety and will likely pursue you. Keep in mind that time is on your side. There is no need to respond right away other than to say you will discuss the disagreement later. Remember, time is *definitely* on your side. Your child cannot do anything without you. You have stepped outside the situation and broken the verbal confrontation.

Meanwhile, the child's anxiety starts to rise while he wonders what you are going to do. Think back to the days when your mother threatened to "...tell your father about your behavior when he gets home." Now that was scary! What was dad going to do? No one knew. And you probably avoided finding out by working out a deal with your mother before he got home. You have a new tool. As you come to understand that anxiety is not always bad, you can begin *using anxiety in a positive way.* What would be accomplished without it? Anxiety drives us to get assignments done, bills paid, to work hard, etc. If we didn't have deadlines when would any of us have finished school? (More about the positive use of anxiety later.)

Again, remember to stay in control—and use words! In order to solve any problem, you must first be able to put it into words. If you are unable to verbalize what is bothering you, you cannot understand the problem, let alone solve it. On the other hand, once you put the problem into words, you will begin to find the solution because you have begun to define the problem. You help your child solve problems when you help him put issues into words.

Ask Questions and Think Out Loud

Let us go back to the example of the child in the store with her mother. What if that parent had handled things differently? If a child refuses to answer a parent's questions about what she thinks her temper tantrum behavior will gain, the parent can shift to thinking out loud. The parent can begin by saying, "Let me think out loud about this. If I give in to your demands and your temper tantrum, I am sending you the wrong message. I am sending you the message that the way to get what you want is to have a temper tantrum or refuse to talk until you get what you want. Now that seems like a dangerous precedent to set for the both of us. On the other hand, if I do not give in, you might continue to act out and that would not be good."

Step back a little and let the situation slow down. You may continue to say, "You know you are a smart person and I'm sure you can understand that if there's any chance for this to work out, we'll have to go home and talk it through." By saying this, you're trying to shape the child's perception of the here and now. To the child this may be an absolute (always was and always will be) situation rather than a relative (it had a beginning and it will have an end) situation.

With this approach, several things can happen. The child may see that she is being outrageous and decide that if she has any chance of winning, she must appear reasonable and be willing to talk about the problem. There is also the other possibility that the child does not want to give up her perceived moment of triumph and advantage—and will decide to continue to press the issue.

If your child chooses the first option, she should be congratulated for her willingness to understand and cooperate. Don't go overboard with your praise, a simple "You made a good choice." will work effectively. By offering a few words of praise about your child's good decision, you're working on helping her shape her narrative about herself. You want your child to understand that being reasonable is part of her DNA.

However, if your child chooses the second option of stay and fight, you may have to shift the focus more toward consequences. You might say something like, "You know we will have to go home sometime—whether that is now or later—and when we do, we will revisit this incident and figure out how to handle situations like this for the future when we're out in public. If it takes us fifteen minutes or thirty minutes or an hour to reach some kind of an agreement, you will owe me time. It will have to be paid back. Let me just advise you that the time you will need to pay back may well occur at a time that is inconvenient for you. It may be a time when you want to go out with a friend or go to a movie or whatever. Now I am going to give you some space and stand over by the door while you make a decision."

By doing this, you're attempting to use anxiety in a positive way. If you never have used this strategy before, your child may not understand that you will follow through. If that is the case, your child may or may not believe you. However, if you employ the strategy once—and you follow through—your child is very likely to believe you for the future. If you have to use this approach and you follow through, you're helping to ensure not only a positive resolution of the current difficulty; but also, you're setting up all future situations to be resolved in a more positive manner.

Avoiding the double bind, and using a situation as a teaching moment, is up to the parent. Not only do you have a chance to turn a potentially bad situation into a positive situation, it is also an opportunity to influence the child's self-narrative. You want your child to believe that she is capable of being reasonable under stress. Your child's self-concept and self-esteem will continue to evolve all as a function of the moving target that you deal with on a day-to-day basis.

Chapter 6 Questions

Do I need to learn new skills and how to use them effectively?

Do I hear myself raising my voice when I am upset?

Am I putting myself into a self-imposed double bind?

Do I realize being in control gets more attention than raising my voice?

Why use words to define situations and not act out on my feelings?

Chapter 7

CLARIFYING ONE'S VALUES: COGNITIVE DISSONANCE VERSUS THE SPIN DOCTOR

We want children to use words for another very important reason, which is to help them understand who they are and what they stand for and believe. We want children to understand what they say about themselves as people. Do people really know what they are thinking about themselves—or do they need help in understanding what they are all about? Research from neuroscience would say no. Studies indicate that others know us better than we know ourselves. Sometimes others can reveal what is going on within us better than we can.

Lessons from History
From time to time, a person comes along and puts what he believes into words in a way that people understand, identify with and make their own. One of these persons was Thomas Paine when he wrote the famous *Common Sense*. Paine brilliantly and succinctly summarized the colonial cause in a way that people understood and believed. He spoke to a place that was inside the common man about the principles of democracy in such a way that his words resonated. Paine was able to express what people were saying unconsciously to themselves.

Abraham Lincoln used this innate talent when he gave the Gettysburg Address. Many people in the work-weary North wanted an end to the war and bloodshed. Lincoln concisely stated the importance of preserving the Union within the context of the great experiment of democracy. He gave meaning to the suffering. These two men were able to understand what was inside the minds and hearts of others better than their listeners knew.

Does Looking Inside Ourselves to Know Who We Are Work?

Studies from neuroscience indicate it may be fruitless to try to look solely within ourselves to understand who we are and why we do what we do. The reason for this is we may well believe a myth we have created about ourselves. If looking inward is not reliable—can looking outward at our behavior and what others say about us help establish a better personal narrative? Following this model, it is important to look at our behavior from the viewpoint of how others react to us to get a better understanding of our actions. Children are especially vulnerable to misunderstanding what their behavior is saying about whom they are and what their values really are.

What gets in our way of understanding ourselves? The answer lies in our ability to rationalize our behavior. Each of us has his very own spin doctor—the self-protective mechanism of our mind that justifies our behavior and allows us to spin actions and situations in the most favorable light possible. An excellent example of how we are able to rationalize can be found in the film *Thank You for Smoking*. In this film, Nick Naylor (Aaron Eckhart) is a lobbyist defending Big Tobacco. One situation follows another in which Nick seems hopelessly trapped by the role he has chosen. How can he possibly view himself in a positive light? Yet, each time Nick appears trapped, he is able to spin the story to come out on top.

Nick's son, Joey, lives with his mother. When Nick is invited to speak to Joey's class about his job, we can see Joey visible cringe—his father is going to defend tobacco to his classmates? When Nick is asked a question about the evils of smoking, he almost effortlessly shifts the topic and makes it one of freedom to choose rather than the effects of tobacco on health. Afterwards, trying to remain a role model for his twelve-year-old son, Nick explains to Joey that if you argue correctly, you are never wrong. Nick is so successful in teaching his son this lesson that in one scene, Joey is able to get his mother to change her mind and allows Joey to go on a business trip to California with his father. Joey manipulates his mother by asking her if her initial refusal to let him go on a trip with his father is her way of taking her frustration of a failed marriage out on him. The scene ends with the boy getting in the car to head off to California with his father.

While unrealistic, we can enjoy the cleverness with which Nick Naylor can turn virtually every situation to his advantage including his own near-death experience from a nicotine overdose. As Nick is in recovery from the drug's toxicity, he proclaims that it is his heavy use of tobacco that saved his life. Nick claims that it is his career as a smoker that allowed him to build up such a high tolerance. Nick Naylor is not alone—there is a spin doctor in all of us that allows us to justify almost any behavior.

Cognitive Dissonance: The Counterbalance to the Spin Doctor

Cognitive dissonance is defined as the psychological conflict resulting from simultaneously held incongruous beliefs and attitudes. The concept was introduced by psychologist Leon Festinger (1919–1989) in the late 1950s. Dr. Festinger and later researchers showed that when confronted with challenging new information, most people seek to preserve their current understanding of the world by rejecting, explaining away, or avoiding the new information—or by convincing themselves that no conflict exists. Cognitive dissonance is considered an explanation for attitude change.

Organization Occurs at Output. Why Is It Important to Get a Child to Talk?

Getting in touch with our values is vital: The only way we really get in touch with our values is to state them in a variety of situations, to add in to what others say about us...to observe how others react to us and to listen to contradictions as they arise about our values. (Back to Socrates and his method.) Is it necessary to state values in order to understand them? Yes. Expressing our values forces us to organize what we believe. Simply stated: Organization occurs at output. If the child does not have to talk, thoughts and values will probably not be formulated. One the other hand, if the child is encouraged to talk and does so, his thoughts and values will be formulated.

If we believe what neuroscientists tell us about most of our actions coming as a result of habit patterns, it follows that most people do not stop to think about their values and why they do what they do. This does not mean that the individual does not have values; it may just mean that the values get lost when the individual does not verbalize what the value is and how it applies in specific circumstances.

To understand how behavior and values can be affected by circumstances, you only have to look to the Stanford prison experiment led by psychology professor, Phillip Zimbardo from August 14-20, 1971. Twenty-four male undergraduate students with no known psychological issues were selected to take part in the study. The participants were divided into two groups to play the role of either guard or prisoner in a simulated prison in the basement of the Stanford Psychology building. As the study progressed, the group that role-played guards became increasingly abrasive and abusive. The group that played the role of prisoners became submissive and depressed. As the guards enforced authoritarian measures—and, in some cases psychological torture—many of the prisoners passively accepted the abuse and at the request of the guards, harassed fellow prisoners who attempted to prevent it because they were experiencing extreme stress. The study, which was to run for two weeks, was abruptly discontinued after six days because of the emotional effects it was having on the participants—including Zimbardo who in his role of superintendent had permitted the abuse to continue.

Later, in reviewing their behavior, most of the guards found it difficult to reconcile what they believed with how badly they had behaved. Likewise, the prisoners found it difficult to believe that they had responded with such submissive behavior in the face of authority. It was an awakening for all the participants. The relevance of the study reemerged when acts of prison torture and abuse at the Abu Ghraib prison in Iraq became known March 2001.

In the face of circumstances, the participants of the Stanford prison experiment seemed to have lost their way—as well as their values. What might have happened had the prisoners and guards been able to "step back" and examine their behavior in light of their stated values? The prisoners and guards, after accepting the roles they were to play, simply seemed to go on automatic pilot—they stopped thinking about their values almost completely until they could no longer avoid doing so as a result of the emotional trauma that was created.

Words Are Important

When I listen better, the other person has to think more about what is being said. I want the other person to speak without interruption because I want them to hear what they are saying. When I speak, I have to *organize* my thoughts, *modify* my language to avoid saying something stupid and I *believe* what I am saying because I hear myself saying it.

When you are listening, at the conclusion of your child speaking, you can say "Let me see if I understand you." Go back to the principles of negotiation outlined in Chapter 3. If you present your child's position in the best and most accurate fashion so your child knows you understand, you can begin to identify what sounds like inconsistencies and ask your child to explain. Have you ever noticed how teachers always sound so smart? Teachers have to *organize* material in order to teach effectively because organization occurs at output. Whatever they teach, when they do it over and over again, it becomes a part of them.

When we listen to a child and ask questions about what they are saying, we are helping them organize their thinking. As we continue to ask questions, they continue to *modify* what they believe and finally—and hopefully—they now *believe* it because they hear themselves saying it.

Cognitive Dissonance Is Central to Creating an Environment of Trust

If you are interested in knowing why getting your child to verbalize his values works, understanding cognitive dissonance is key. Cognitive dissonance is central to many forms of persuasion to change beliefs, values, attitudes, and behaviors. People do not like to say something if it is against their beliefs. As a result, rather than say something they do not believe, people will often avoid answering questions directly or not at all. Instead, they will talk around the topic while trying to explain away any threat to their belief.

Let's look at an example of cognitive dissonance. There is a famous study of cognitive dissonance in which a teacher conspired with a class to highlight the effect of cognitive dissonance. Before the last student came into class, the teacher arranged with all of the other students to give a wrong answer to a question that he would ask. After giving the answer, the teacher would confirm that the *incorrect* answer was correct. The only one not in on the conspiracy was the missing student. When the last student was present and the class had begun, the teacher asked the question to which all of the student conspirators gave the wrong answer. A video recording picked up the smirk on the victim student's face when he first heard the wrong answer. He looked stunned when the teacher affirmed that the answer was correct. The teacher then began calling on a few other students, all of whom gave the incorrect answer. Finally, the teacher called on the victim student who, by this time, had developed all sorts of tics and twitches. The victim student obviously did not want to give the wrong answer because he knew the correct answer. After an obvious physical struggle, he caved in and also gave the wrong answer.

The point is—when someone has to say something that he knows to be not true—it is not done easily. Often it is so difficult to do that physical manifestations give the person away.

Get a "Yes" or "No" at the Outset

When you ask questions, it is important to get a "yes" or "no" at the outset before you listen to an explanation. An answer to any question should not start with an explanation followed by a "yes" or a "no." The purpose for this is to put limitations on your child's internal spin doctor. Following this approach, conclusions are reached more efficiently and frustration is minimized.

Once a question is asked, the possibility of cognitive dissonance arises, often recognizable by the discomfort a person shows when he is uncomfortable with something he is saying. The person not being honest or being evasive frequently develops visible indicators like tics or twitches (a "tell" sign, as it's called in Texas Hold 'Em poker). Couples can frequently tell their partner's reactions to situations simply by picking up on subtle signs of pleasure or displeasure. If the person being questioned is not being forthright, honest, and open, asking questions and waiting for direct answers builds cognitive dissonance.

Cognitive Dissonance Can Be a Motivator to Change

Cognitive dissonance is a very important motivator to create change. When children say something that they do not believe, anxiety is created. The resulting dissonance or discomfort feels like a tension between the two opposing thoughts. To release the tension one of three actions can be taken:

- Change behavior. ("I think I will do it a different way.")
- Justify behavior by changing thoughts about what is proper.

- Justify behavior by adding different ideas. ("I had not thought of that before.")

Whichever action your child chooses to take, change is going to happen because your child has to confront his own value system and the resulting action must be in harmony with that value system.

Can Someone Be Honest and Not Honest at the Same Time?

Sometimes, children answer questions with the intention to mislead, staying just within the bounds of what might be considered honest. They are being honest but not open. The person who is honest but not open is trying to manage the news to get the results he wants. When someone is open, that person does not edit the information. The person gives the information freely and speaks without hesitation.

Children will sometimes hedge on the truth especially if doing so would result in loss of some freedom. The issue of openness versus truthfulness should be addressed with a child. The parent thinks out loud, "You want me to trust you and I want to trust you. If you answer my questions fully by volunteering information that would be relative to your safety that will help make me trust you. If your behavior is always consistent with your word, I will trust you; I would have no other choice. So let me ask you again, are you being open?"

Chapter 7 Questions

Am I asking my child to explain his/her values?

Am I creating an environment of trust?

Do I insist on a "yes" or "no" at the outset of the answer when asking a value question?

Am I making cognitive dissonance work for me?

Chapter 8

THE ROAD TO COMPETENCY:

ACQUIRING THE TOOLS

In order to build anything as complex as a relationship, one must first acquire the tools and then learn to use the tools well. The good news is that the tools can be described and can be learned; the bad news is that using them effectively takes time and practice. The reason it takes time to learn has to do with you doing something unfamiliar—you have not made it part of you yet. The other reason it takes time is your child's reluctance or resistance to going along with the changes you are making. As the parent, competency will come if you persist. Competency arises though practice—doing the right thing over and over again until it becomes part of your adaptive unconscious.

In a sense, some of the approaches outlined to treat dysfunction and build relationships can seem like a cookbook approach with recipes for a variety of different dishes or different situations. It may be read and used as a cookbook and that might work fine. However, the approaches discussed are intended to be more than a question and answer recipe to specific situations. The focus in examining these situations is on the *how* and *why* changes can and do take place.

The personal part of the equation in the use of the tools is that the tools become most effective when they are in the hands of the competent parent. To be really successful on an ongoing basis and not just in one crisis intervention, a parent will have to make internal changes to become more competent. Change is almost never easy, especially when it comes to overcoming old habits based on past behavior—while changing over to a more thoughtful, considered approach. The other part of the equation is your child's reaction. He may not like the changes you are trying to impose. Change for your child can mean more work and less fun. He is not likely to want to invest in your new approach and may well resist both actively or passively. It is going to take time to convince your child that the changes are here to stay. This is where perseverance comes into play.

Get Started: Make the Vocabulary (the "Buzzwords") a Part of You
Behavioral principles will be described and applied to various situations that arise between parent and child. The strategies and tools needed to deal with your child in a variety of situations are best seen in the context of examples. To really understand why these principles work, you need to learn the strategies and the reasons behind the prescriptions.

Words from communication theory like meta-communication, paradox and double bind will be used over and over again. It will take time and practice to become familiar with these words and even more time to feel comfortable enough to use the strategies behind the words in effective ways. Actually, you have probably already used a number of these strategies, maybe without knowing the vocabulary—and if you used them, you may have done so in both a strategic and haphazard way. Hopefully, you will see yourself in many of the situations I describe and you can begin to see how the approaches may be used. Once you have learned and employed the techniques listed here, life at home will become a good deal easier.

It will take practice. You must go step by step…until you do it almost automatically…until you get into the state that has been described as Four Stages for Learning Any New Skill and The Conscious Competence Learning Model. The model has been attributed to several sources including Gordon Training International Organization and to psychologist, Abraham Maslow (although it is not found in his writings). More recently Joseph O'Connor and John Seymour, authors of *Introducing NLP: Psychological Skills for Understanding and Influencing People* have called it the Zone.

The Zone: You Will Know It When You Get There

There are four steps to the Zone as it has been described in the literature:

1. Unconsciously Incompetent: When one begins anything new, you are at the first step. You are unconsciously incompetent. You are so incompetent you do not know just how incompetent you are. Remember the first time you tried to play a sport or master skiing or a dance step? You were such a mess you did not even know how much of a mess you were—how could you? You were looking only at your feet. Others may have looked at you and smiled as though enjoying your seemingly feeble attempts to learn while perhaps remembering that is how they got started.

2. Consciously Incompetent: Through practice, you get a little better but are now aware of how incompetent you are and wonder to yourself if you should continue to learn because it takes a good deal of work and thinking. You will have to fight off the tendency to think, "I will never learn this." If you believe you cannot do something, you probably will not be able to. Instead, you must keep at it. It will come and you must persist.

3. Consciously Competent: You realize that practice is paying off and that you can do it. You may find yourself giving a few words of advice to other parents, who are now starting to think of you as brilliant. Do not let it go to your head. There is still much to learn and the situations will keep changing.

4. Unconsciously Competent: You are in the Zone. You are so good at it, you do not have to stop and think. You're there!

Does this mean that you will no longer make mistakes? No. You will continue to encounter new situations that will give you pause but with practice, you will recover faster.

Whenever we watch a professional in action, we are usually struck by how easy she makes it look. That's why we call them professionals. Is it easy? No. If it were easy, everyone would be doing it. It takes practice. Take control of yourself first and then remember…practice…practice…practice.

Learning and applying the vocabulary of psychology to unlock the intricacies and interactions of human behavior is key. Remember, everything new starts with learning the concepts and vocabulary. Every new subject you learned in school, from science to literature started as a language course. If it was math, you had to learn what the word *fraction* meant before you could work with them. If it was chemistry, you had to learn what the words *atom* and *molecule meant,* or if it was history, what a *timeline* is.

Paradox and Reverse Psychology

Paradox is a self-contradictory statement whose underlying meaning is understood only by careful examination. Often, it is a direction to produce an opposite or counterintuitive result. Its purpose is to get a person to view a situation differently.

The goal for the child in any paradoxical situation is to set up the circumstance so that the child "makes him" do what is right despite whatever reservations the child might have about doing so. The purpose of paradox is to make the child thoughtful about his behavior before the child engages in it. The parent needs to be prepared for the resulting negative behavior so that there is no surprise or acting out of expression of anger on the part of the child. After all, the parent has given permission for the behavior that he does not want, so the parent's response must be under control. By using this strategy, the parent can continue to express love and concern without making things worse.

Paradoxical Techniques Can Overcome Temper Tantrums

John is a young boy who typically has a temper tantrum when he is told about a plan to go with the family to visit a relative. His parents, anticipating a temper tantrum when it is time to leave can say, "You often have a temper tantrum when you don't like something that we have to do and that delays us getting started. We have to leave in a few minutes so why don't you have a temper tantrum now and get it out of the way."

At this point, if the child has a temper tantrum, he is conforming to his parents' request. The whole value of the temper tantrum has been lost—and the child will probably not have a temper tantrum. But, even if the child does have the tantrum, the child is still doing what the parent asked.

Let's Look at an Example of Paradox and Its Integration into Negotiation

Paradox has been used time and again in film but perhaps nowhere more effectively than in the classic 1960s Western *Butch Cassidy and the Sundance Kid.* In the opening scene, the Sundance Kid (Robert Redford) is playing a card game. Suddenly one of the gamblers steps away from the table accusing Sundance of cheating and tells him to leave the money on the table and walk away. There is immediate tension with all the makings of a classic barroom gunfight to ensue. At that point Butch Cassidy, played by Paul Newman, attempts to mediate between the two men. With neither man willing to budge, Butch Cassidy turns to the Sundance Kid and says, "There's nothing more I can do for you, Sundance." The other gunfighter, hearing the name Sundance and apparently knowing of the man's reputation, abruptly is made aware that if he engages in a gunfight, he has only a short time to live. The gunfighter turns to Butch Cassidy and asks, "What should I do?" Butch Cassidy replies, "Invite him to stay, then he will go." The gunfighter turns to the Sundance Kid and says, "Can you stay and play a few more hands, Kid?" The Sundance Kid rising from the table says, "No thanks, I've got to be going." As Sundance speaks, he scoops the money into his hat and leaves with Butch Cassidy. The paradox is that the only way to get Sundance to leave was to invite him to stay.

In another example from the same film, Butch Cassidy and the Sundance Kid find themselves trapped on a mountain, surrounded by lawmen who are determined to bring the outlaws to justice. With no apparent way to escape, Butch Cassidy sees a fast-moving river and suggests to Sundance that they jump into the river and swim away from the law. At first, Sundance refuses. When Butch Cassidy presses him as to why he does not want to seize this chance for freedom, Sundance replies that he cannot swim. Butch immediately reframes the situation using paradox and assures Sundance not to worry about being able to swim because *the fall will kill him*. Next, we see the fellow outlaws jump together into the river.

For our current purposes and at its simplest definition, paradox can be used as a parenting technique to short-circuit a child's resistance. Basically, the parent does something that sounds contradictory to what he actually wants. Instead of telling the child to do something the child does not want to do, the parent directs the child to continue doing a negative behavior. The use of paradox places the parent back in control because whatever the child does, the parent gave the direction—and the only way for the child to disobey is to not have a temper tantrum. Paradox can be difficult to master because it almost always borders on sarcasm and use of sarcasm can make any potentially bad situation worse.

Nearly everyone has had the experience of watching someone who is very agitated pace around the room. There is the tendency to want to help the person by saying "Calm down. Sit down and relax." This may work on occasion. However, generally it is not a good approach. If the person could relax, he certainly would not be pacing about the room. If fact, if you were to say "Calm down," it is likely you might well produce the opposite effect. The person may become more agitated.

Instead, it would be better to say, "That's it, keep pacing. It will allow you to burn off some of that energy until you're ready to sit down." One thing we can be sure of, the person pacing will eventually get tired enough to sit down as long as we do not say anything to fuel the person's upset. The direction to calm *yourself and sit down* probably will have the opposite effect. The helper may be met with an angry outburst. "Mind your own business!"

A case example: On an initial interview, a parent showed up for an appointment accompanied by his teenage son. Both of them looked a little disheveled. The father explained he had just that morning ordered his son to go to his room for talking back (control). When the son refused to comply, the father became more strident in his demand for compliance. Still, the son refused to go to his room (resistance). The father, seeing no alternative, described his response to the rebellious behavior, as "I had to put him in his room."

A physical struggle ensued with the son finally being *put* in his room. The son was a rather well-developed teenager, about the same height as his father. And, if anyone knows anything about teenagers, they are strong and usually more physically fit than the parents.

When the son was questioned if his father had really put him in his room, he replied, "Sort of." When questioned further, the son expanded to say that his father had only been successful because he had given up toward the end because, "I was afraid my father would have a heart attack."

Upset that the question was asked of his son, the father turned to me, "Why did you ask him that? Now my son thinks he can win." It was pointed out that his son did think he could fight but stopped out of concern that his father would have a heart attack.

The father was instructed not to put his hands on or fight with his son in the future but simply tell him to go to his room. "What if he refuses?" was the father's immediate response. He was advised that if his son were to refuse to go to his room (resistance), the father should say, "That's okay, you do not have to go right away." Apply the use of paradox and allow the child to continue his behavior. "Go when you want but just know that you will owe me time. Whatever length of time it takes you to get to your room will have to be repaid when you are ready to come back and talk with me." Without saying it the son is given the chance to get himself under control. "When you come back, I will expect an apology, an explanation of how you will handle situations like this for the future, and a suggestion of a positive behavior to take the place of the negative behavior. Take your time. Go when you want and let me know when you are ready to talk. In the meantime, I'll run the clock."

Keep the Choice Simple: Avoid Arguing
Parents should not be in the business of rewarding argumentative behavior. By allowing your child to go to his room when he decides to do so, you are putting your child theoretically in the driver's seat. The child decides when the punishment will start and when the punishment will end. In this way, giving the child a choice ends the argument.

There Are Two Gains in Using Paradox in Conjunction with the 3 Strategies Approach:
1. Immediate gain in which you arrest and change the behavior; and
2. Longer-term gain in which you reinforce change for the future as the child learns what will happen going forward in similar situations.

In order to understand how this works in practice, let us continue with the young man who refused to go to his room when directed to do so by his father.

There Is a Lot to Be Learned in Understanding the Elements of an Apology

During the therapeutic session, the son is told that when he comes back to talk it out with his father, he will be required to apologize with an apology consisting of several elements:

1. An acknowledgment of the behavior and an expression of sorrow for the behavior;

    (It can be a simple, "I'm sorry I reacted the way I did.")

2. A statement of how similar situations will be handled in the future,

    (The child outlines what he will do for the future—after all, isn't doing things right the best way to apologize?);

3. Make amends and be ready to do a positive behavior to take the place of the negative behavior.

The session ended when the situation appeared to be resolved. Two days later the father called pleading, "I've got to see you right away." After stating that he was not in crisis, he was scheduled for the early afternoon. At the appointed time, the father rushed into my office, sat down and told me that he had ordered his son to his room. When the son refused, the father followed the instructions that I had given to him the previous day. To the amazement of the father, his son immediately got up and went to his room! The father asked me, "Why does it work?"

Why Does It Work?

The first thing the parent did was to change the nature of the confrontation from an external ("It's you or me, pal, and I am ready to fight.") to an internal conflict (the child has no one to fight with in his room; the child has only the clock with which to argue and clocks do not argue back). With time, the son internalized the conflict, accepted responsibility, and ultimately decided on a negotiation approach. Negotiation can begin once a child gives an apology. But, negotiation must first start with an apology.

Remember, the apology does a number of things: It acknowledges and corrects bad behavior to good behavior and, maybe even more important—it decreases the likelihood that such confrontations will take place in the future. The child will not want to go through it again—and probably neither will you.

External Versus Internal Conflict

When it comes to taking responsibility, all conflicts have a significant internal component.

How many times have you heard your child say about a teacher, "My teacher flunked me!" You may even have said something like that yourself when you were in school and hoped your parents would buy your explanation for your lack of success. Of course, the teacher would probably see it differently and say something like, "I didn't flunk you, I grade tests and report grades. The grade you earned was in the failing range. You failed. I merely reported the grade."

This type of response places the burden back on the shoulders of the student where it belongs. An appropriate question from the parent to the child is: "What can you do differently for the future?" Just like the teacher in this example, the parent should be very reluctant to assume the role of the bad guy.

A parent's job is to get his child to assume responsibility for behavior, not evade or blame someone else. Getting a child to focus on what he *did* or *did not do* and what he *should do* or *not do* best accomplishes this.

If your child attempts to shift the focus to you, by saying "You're too strict! No one else's parents expect what you expect," don't let yourself fall into the trap and start defending. If you do, you will find yourself drawn into a confrontation you cannot win. You will lose because you gave control to the child. The focus belongs inside the child.

Let's revisit the father and son example. As long as the son could keep the conflict external through a face-to-face confrontation his father, the son could continue to resist. Once the external conflict was made internal by using paradox, the situation changed. The son was in a position to begin and therefore end the punishment whenever he wanted. It was up to him. Once in his room, the young man had only the clock with which to contend. The son could glare at the clock and shake his fist but a clock does not respond. The ticking clock kept reminding the son of the time he was wasting by just sitting in his room.

By the father telling his son to begin when he wanted, the child was seemingly in the driver's seat—but not really. The son was only in the position of both starting and ending potential punishment before he could begin the negotiation.

There Is a Need for an Apology

No apology is complete with just "I'm sorry." It is a *starting point—not an endpoint*—and it should be accepted without challenging how sincere the child sounds. Often, a parent who is angry with his child might respond with "Well, you don't sound very sorry to me." It really should not be about how sincere or insincere the child appears to be. What you are trying to achieve beyond this incident is to create a pattern for helping your child take responsibility for his behavior—now *and* for the future. "I'm sorry" is a good beginning.

But, why is the child sorry? Is he sorry for getting caught or for doing something wrong? To correct a behavior, your child needs to apologize for a specific behavior as part of a multiple-step process. It's not as easy as merely saying, "I'm sorry, I shouldn't have thrown my phone down. I'm sorry it's broken but I was angry." When your child tries to excuse his behavior by saying he was angry, he has not learned the correct way to handle anger. Being angry does not give one license to act out. This leads to the second part of the apology—the *identification* of the behavior that must be changed.

At this point, your child will often want to get into a lengthy explanation of why he responded as he did—and in a sense excuse his poor behavior—because of how he felt at that moment. If you allow your child to retell the event, the chances are great that your child will become angrier because he will be focused on what upset him. Instead of going into the incident *directly*, approach it *indirectly*. In lieu of a question like "Why did you do that?"—ask your child to identify a better way to handle similar situations going forward. Continue with "Rather than the angry way you just responded, tell me what you could have done differently and, how you intend to handle this kind of incident for the future." Implicit in any explanation of how your child will handle problems for the future is an admission of what he has done wrong in the present. It is more important and productive to then focus your child on how to handle anger in the future rather than go back over what went wrong in the past.

With this approach, your child will learn to formulate a different way of dealing with his anger so that it does not result in aggressive behavior. *Anger is a feeling—aggression is a behavior.* While the child may have no control over how he feels at the moment, he must be taught to gain control over his response to his feelings and behave appropriately. By giving your child the chance to talk about future behavior, you have succeeded in focusing your child on how to do something correctly.

The next step of an apology has to do with your child demonstrating that he has learned from his mistake so that he can consistently cope with upsetting circumstances better for the future. You might say something like, "I want to be sure you really understand the importance of handling your feelings properly. Are you willing to describe future upsetting situations and how you will manage them?" By doing this, you encourage your child to verbalize how he is processing problems while at the same time praising your child and building a positive and stronger relationship between the two of you.

The last step of an apology is making amends. It could be doing extra chores around the house, volunteering to do community service or finding a way to pay for something that your child has damaged during a temper tantrum. Making amends is vital for the healing process—and, because it is the acknowledgment of responsibility to others.

Ask Questions, Think Out Loud, and Tell Stories: What Is the Value of This Approach?

Suppose we apply the approach of asking questions, thinking out loud, and telling stories. The parent can say, "Let's think about this. I asked you to go to your room and think about what you have done and you refuse to go. Now, there are a number of options. You could continue to refuse or you could do what I ask. If you refuse, this problem will not simply go away. You will have to eventually go along or your world will come to a pause, if not a stop, in terms of enjoying more freedom. However, if you do as you're told, this problem can be resolved rather quickly. You're a smart person. Give it some thought. I'm sure you can see the importance of working this out. Take your time. Think about it. What is the really smart way to handle this problem?"

Is this approach the same as the first solution? Yes, as far as the paradox and result but with a subtle difference of laying out the options—thinking out loud, presenting both sides of what can happen, and asking questions. "What is the smart thing to do here? You're a smart person. We have been able to work out things like this in the past. Do you remember (tell a story about a situation that worked out well) and how you solved it? That worked, because you did the smart thing." This approach works in the here and now but it also has long-range effects for the future.

Teach the Other Person to Negotiate: Why Do We Want to Do That?

We want our children to learn how to negotiate and present their ideas clearly and hopefully, in a dispassionate way. You should want your child to come forward with a proposal that reflects goals and values. It should be pointed out to the child that the manner of presentation is almost as important as what the child wants. "Tell me what you want and what steps you plan to take to ensure a safe outcome."

Guide your child through this learning process because when a child talks, three things happen. The child has to:

1. *Organize* his thoughts in order to state values,
2. *Modify* what he is saying as he is talking because no one wants to sound stupid,
3. *Believe* because he hears himself saying it in his own words.

Give your child a chance to hear his inconsistencies. It will also give you a chance to talk through the inconsistencies. When your child is finished, repeat what you think your child has heard and ask him to agree about what has been decided. If you do, you will lock in the new, improved behavior in place of the previous behavior. "So you're saying that you recognize the need for improvement and you agree to handle situations like this differently in the future. Isn't that right?" When the child agrees, the parent confirms the choice once again, "Good, I think you handled that well." You have rewarded good behavior and not become the punisher of bad behavior!

Chapter 8 Questions

Am I working toward getting "in the zone"?

Am I able to use paradox effectively?

Am I asking for the right kind of an apology?

Am I teaching my child to apologize and negotiate?

Chapter 9

THE FAMILY MEETING—THE VALUE OF THE SHARED NARRATIVE— OVERCOMING THE RESISTANCE TO MEET: I DON'T LIKE CONFRONTATION!

Family meetings in the history of film and theater have often been portrayed as dramatic moments filled with heightened tension and confrontation. In some films, such as the Academy Award–winning 1980 film *Ordinary People*, denial and avoidance are at the heart of the conflict that threatens to divide the family. The family is torn apart following the accidental death of the older son and the attempted suicide by the younger son. Mary Tyler Moore won the Academy Award for her portrayal of the bitter mother who wants to move on and maintain an appearance of the perfect family without dealing with the feelings of hurt experienced by her husband and son. The mother believes she has moved on and healed herself and cannot understand why others cannot do the same without talking about the event and its impact on the family.

At the other end of the spectrum is the theatrical production *God of Carnage* (made into a film titled *Carnage*). This is a story of what can go wrong when two well-intentioned sets of parents agree to meet for a civilized discussion following the aftermath of the assault on one child by the other child. What starts out as a respectful, intelligent exchange of ideas rapidly slips into irrational arguments filled with hostility and bitterness. Perhaps this is the type of exchange that many people fear and is what prevents them from coming together as a family to focus on positives and healing.

Meetings Have Value

Despite the sometimes-negative portrayal of family meetings, the question remains—do family meetings have a value in creating and maintaining a positive family narrative. Family meetings provide an opportunity for the individual members to step back, pause and reflect on their various interactions within the family. It provides family members with a chance to support one another while helping to reframe and reinterpret individual interactions. The goal is always to increase communication and support through respectful listening.

Personal Narrative Dictates Interaction and Allows Perspective

Each family member's perception of himself is rooted in personal narrative—the story he believes about himself—whether he is feeling loved and appreciated or whether he is feeling discounted and picked on. The individual's personal narrative will dictate how he interacts without family members and others. The meeting provides the opportunity to step back and allow perspective on what is happening. It allows for story editing so that an individual can make sense of an event that perhaps was misinterpreted initially. It provides the opportunity to label behavior in a positive way. Perhaps most important, it allows and encourages sustained change in perception and reinforces new behaviors. At the heart of the meeting is the encouragement of storytelling—encouraging the child to tell how he has changed and discuss how much better he feels as a result of the change.

Family Narrative Is a Useful Tool in Creating Understanding

Families create a narrative about themselves as a group just as the individual members create narratives about themselves. Family meetings give individuals a chance to understand and integrate life experiences into both the family narrative and the individual narrative. As neuroscience has demonstrated, others often know us better than we know ourselves. So, too, the family as a whole is often able to understand the individual in a more clear and precise light than the individual can accomplish by himself. To understand how a family meeting can be integrated into a useful tool, let us look at a potentially dangerous situation that can be processed and handled later by family members.

A Behavior Problem in the Car Illustrates the Need for a Family Intervention

The family car is a potential battleground. There is much to like about being in a car and driving with one's children. Parents often comment about the willingness of their children to open up and talk more freely when they're in the car than when they're at home. Invariably, parents wonder what is it about this environment that allows their children to become more chatty and open. If they were to ask their children why that is—as I have done with many children—they might discover that children believe the car is the one place they are safe to say anything without worrying about their parents freaking out. Children tend to feel freer to act out with one another knowing that their parents will be more restricted to intervene. As a result, children often feel more free to express themselves. This can result in serious distraction for the parent behind the wheel.

Distractions caused by unruly behavior in the car can have significant implications with regard to risk. Obviously, the openness the child feels to communicate in the car has its benefits. However, there is a potential strong downside to the child feeling empowered to speak his mind in the perceived safety of the car. Children have come to realize that their parents are relatively helpless to do anything but drive if they hope to get to their destination safely. The parent must maintain control or risk an accident. The one thing a parent cannot do when children act out in the car is to become agitated and distracted. What happens when the child turns nasty and demanding or starts a fight with a sibling?

What to Do?

Most parents would probably not be feeling very calm if their child was to act out in the car but there are things you can do to bring the crisis under control.

Ask a question. Ask your child in as calm a voice as possible whether he is able to get himself under control—and if not, you can say something like, "If you cannot control yourself and get along with each other, we will have to have a meeting and deal with this issue of safety in the car when we get home. Would you rather try to work things out here and now...or later at a meeting at home?"

If you have a few family meetings under your belt, the threat of a meeting should have a calming effect. Most children do not like the idea of having a meeting in which other family members will be present. The child will be placed in the position to explain his behavior and, more important, to tell you what he will do in the future. Whether a child likes the idea of having a family meeting so he can tell his side of the story—or wants to avoid it—bringing up the topic of a family meeting can be very effective. The threat of an impending meeting employs the use of a little positive anxiety. The child will recognize that a meeting, after you arrive home, will be cutting into his leisure time. As a result of the threat, one of the following outcomes may happen:

1. If the child calms down, s/he should be thanked for listening while you think out loud "That is a good choice and it is important because good passengers make for good drivers when that time comes."

2. If the child does not calm down, the parent can say, "I'm going to have to pull over to the side of the road because this is a potentially dangerous situation. Do you want me to pull over or can you get yourself under control?" Thinking out loud, you can add, "It is dangerous to drive when I am distracted and I do not want you to think it is right to do that."

But, what happens if this does not work, either? Pull over to the side of the road and think out loud to inform the child—or children—that one of two things can happen. "Let me think out loud about this situation. One, you can calm down and we will continue the trip. Or two, if you cannot behave appropriately we will sit in the car until you are under control before we proceed. What would you like to have happen?"

If you have to stop to get order, you should do so. However, if you really must get to your destination, continue the drive but with the warning that "We will deal with the issue of behavior in the car when we get home." This gives the child a chance to think over the possible consequences to his behavior and perhaps decide to become more cooperative. It also introduces the use of positive anxiety as an aid in getting cooperation.

Speaking to the children you say "Just know that even if you give me immediate cooperation, you will owe me an apology consisting of three things: 1. "I need to hear you say first, I'm sorry; 2. I will need to know what you will do for the future; and 3. You will need to be prepared to do a positive behavior to make up for the negative car behavior. Do you remember these steps to an apology?"

Immediate cooperation does not have to merit an immediate family meeting but the negative behavior in the car should be an issue for consideration during a future meeting. Remember, if the children calm down in the car, thank them for cooperating but also tell them that since you had to pull over because your verbal warnings were ignored, some discussion will be necessary. The message should be something like, "Because I need your cooperation in the future and because safety is so important, we will have to discuss this situation at home, when everyone can attend." Create a little more positive anxiety by the anticipation of the family meeting. Once, this statement is made, a meeting must be held as soon as arriving home or shortly afterward.

Proper behavior in the car is so important, not just for the now but as a message for the future. Someday your children will be driving. The issue of safe behavior in the car cannot be over-emphasized since unruly behavior in the car is a much too dangerous situation to be ignored.

The Place and the Time Are Important Elements to a Successful Meeting with the Children

As they say in real estate, it's always a question of *location, location, location.* The location sets the tone for the meeting. It should be chosen by the parent and be a place free from distraction. Many times, a parent in an effort to resolve an issue quickly, will go to the child's room. This may work on occasion but it is generally not a good idea. Such a setting gives the child control— it's the child's domain and as such, the child is in charge. At the end of the meeting, the parent must leave or may be ordered out of the room by the child. If the meeting goes well and the parent and child agree, everything is fine. But let's take a look at what may happen if the one-on-one meeting does not go well and the child says, "I don't want to talk about this anymore!" and orders the parent out of his room while refusing to speak.

What is the parent to do? If the parent refuses to leave the room because the meeting is not going well, the child may continue to insist that the parent leave. And if the parent leaves, the child wins—at least for the moment. If the parent refuses to leave the room, the parent is now virtually in the same spot as in a previous example where the child was ordered to go to his room. The child can win by simply doing nothing while the parent fumes in frustration. Does this sound reminiscent of the double bind? Remember, it is okay to make a mistake. You can recover later.

Okay, the parent made a mistake by trying to hold the meeting in the child's room. The situation can still be salvaged as long as the parent sits back on his skis. The parent can think out loud and say, "I think you need more time to consider your options. I'm going to leave now and I want you to think this over and come to me when you are ready to negotiate. Remember, you will have to give me an apology for your behavior, tell me how you will handle situations like this for the future, and be ready to give me a positive behavior to take the place of the negative behavior you demonstrated. Take your time, let me know when you are ready to talk with me." You have placed the burden back on the child.

This whole situation could possibly have been avoided had the parent chosen a different place for the meeting—a place free from distractions like the family room or the dining room table, which effectively can become the conference room. At the conclusion of the meeting, both parent and child are free to leave.

Who Is in Charge? Let's Take a Look at the Hierarchy of the Family
The parent calls the meeting and sets the rules for discussion. As a parent, it is important to establish that you are in charge. Why? Suppose you want to borrow money from your local bank. Would you call the bank and ask them to send someone to your home or office? Well, you might like to do that but it is highly unlikely that the bank would comply—neither would the IRS if you are asking for personal help with your income tax return. No, those folks would insist you meet at a place they designate just so all the participants know the rules from the outset and who is in charge.

The time of the meeting: In any situation where a meeting is necessary, it should be held as soon as possible after everyone arrives home. In the meantime, the child should be informed that all privileges are suspended until the meeting takes place. The meeting should obviously be done at a time convenient to the parent. Occasionally, the preparation of a meal and meal-time may get in the way of holding an immediate meeting. If this were to occur, the parent should resist all attempts by his child to "...get this over with." Mealtime is for family bonding—not for conducting business that might result in oppositional behavior. Allowing the meeting to take place during a family meal creates conflict instead of harmony. For any meeting to be successful, it is important to remove as many distractions as possible. If a family meeting has to be delayed until after a meal, that is fine—it gives *everyone* more time to think things through and will likely lead to a more efficient conclusion.

How many times has your child handed you a paper to be signed just as the school bus is arriving? Your child insists that you sign the paper right away or he will be late, and the bus is waiting! You do not want to sign the paper because you do not know what you are signing—although you strongly suspect it is not good news. What do you do as your child insists, "There is no time to read it. Just sign it."

Your child has skillfully maneuvered time to his advantage. You could sign the paper, but make it clear that there will be no future signings at the last minute and you want the paper returned at the end of the day for closer examination or you will contact the teacher. Also add, "We will discuss this further when you come home from school today." Do not let your child rush you in any situation.

Structure the Meeting to Keep It As Brief As Possible
The meeting should be scheduled at a time most convenient to the parent. It should be a time convenient to you and perhaps a time less convenient to your child. If the time is less convenient to your child, you will more likely get compliance in less time. Learn from Dr. Skinner's example in Chapter 4: Make the water colder. Let's say you schedule the meeting just before your child's favorite TV show begins. Your child will obviously want to get the meeting over with so he can watch the show.

The meeting should be conducted efficiently but without the aura of being rushed. In addition to handling the present situation, you are trying to set a tone for future meetings. Meetings are important and what is decided at meetings is definitely important. Make it clear to your child that the best way to avoid additional meetings is not to mess up and cause a meeting in the first place. If your child is placing an obstacle in the path of progress by not cooperating, adjourn the meeting and reschedule it for the future.

Opening the meeting and asking questions: The parent must always set the agenda first. The purpose to having a meeting is to get the child to reflect upon his behavior, verbalize what went wrong, take responsibility for his actions, and tell you how he intends to handle things differently for the future. In addition, the child will have to come up with some type of positive behavior to take the place of the negative behavior. If the child is not ready to do this, he should be told, "That's all right, take your time, think about it, and let me know when you want to talk." (This should be starting to sound familiar.) Time is on the side of the parent. Once again, the child is in position of starting and ending what he may view as the punishment.

A reminder: Ask questions, and don't lecture. When your child wants to know what you mean by a positive behavior to take the place of the negative behavior—and asks you what you want him to do—answer the question with a question making sure it is *without any hint of sarcasm*. "I don't know what you could do. You're a smart person. I'm sure you'll figure something out."

Ask Questions and Wait for Answers

If you go first, you will be doing all the work and you have begun bidding against yourself—a no-no in any negotiation. It usually happens that as soon as a parent makes a suggestion, the child says something like "That is too much work. I don't want to do that." At this stage, if you start to give more suggestions, expect them to be shot down and to be left feeling frustrated.

Rather than make a suggestion say, "Take your time and let me know when you come up with something." Now it's your child's meter—not yours—that is running.

What Has Been Gained?

Now, you may be saying that all this is a great deal of work for one incident. Well, that's not exactly true. A lesson has far wider meaning than one specific incident. It all adds up and helps prevent future issues. You're trying to train your child that every time there is an infraction, a rather lengthy (and perhaps somewhat torturous) exercise of having to have a meeting will take place.

At the conclusion of a meeting with your child, you are obviously hoping for an agreement but this might not always be possible. If your child does not work with you to reach an agreement, you can say something like "Take your time, you can start earning rewards again after we negotiate a plan at the next meeting. Let me know when you are ready."

Outline the need for thoughtful consideration as you begin to an adjournment. There is a good chance the child will reconsider his position. Wanting to get back to a TV show, video game, or a phone conversation with a friend usually pressures a child. Time really is on your side; you just need the patience and the will to persist.

Conclude a Meeting on a Positive Note

Your goal is to get participants to verbalize what they have heard and what they believe about themselves within the structure of the family. Remember, you are trying to build an ever-evolving family narrative that is based on positive solutions to situational problems. It is important that each family member views himself as a problem solver.

Use Praise for Good Choices: Never Use Sarcasm

Remember, when the child concedes, praise is in order. Say, "You made a good choice." Never resort to sarcasm. Do not say, "Oh you get it now, do you?" Use of sarcasm can be very damaging, and you risk making situations worse for the future. The child will resent sarcasm and will want to get back at you for using it.

Strive for win-win situations. Resist win-lose situations, which is always the damage of sarcasm. There is no denying that resisting the temptation of use of sarcasm is difficult for many people. Whenever one uses paradox, one is always at the edge of sarcasm. But remember, you can never go over the line or you will lose.

Chapter 9 Questions

Am I handling conflict situations effectively?

Am I paying attention to the place of the meeting?

Am I scheduling the time of the meeting as soon as possible after a conflict?

Am I avoiding lectures, asking questions, telling stories, and thinking out loud?

Chapter 10

AN "EFFECTIVE" PARADIGM INSTEAD OF A "CONSEQUENCE" PARADIGM: OVERCOMING THE CONSEQUENCE MODEL

Perhaps the most difficult part of making changes to your current parenting style is overcoming an old mind-set. Because we are creatures of habit, we tend to revert back to the way we've done things in the past. As a result, people usually are reluctant to change, especially when the change seems radically different from what they are used to doing—even if what they have been doing is not particularly effective. Parents, like children, are trained to respond in a manner consistent with how they were raised. Overcome the old mind-set. If it is not working, find a new way.

There may have been a time in the past when the parent was able to dictate rules and regulations using a heavy-handed style with the threat of possible physical punishment. Faced with the threat of physical punishment, the child usually gave in and did what he was told rather than be subjected to being hit or slapped. Unfortunately, all of this could be done without having to be especially concerned with what others might think or do in response. If there ever was a time when this type of intervention worked, that time has come and gone. People have become more sensitive to the use of physical punishment.

Society has evolved, and the rules have changed with it. Today's home is a far different place although the same challenges remain. Children still rebel and challenge, and parents still have to react and do something about it. While parents may be well trained to do their job at work, their education for home-control methods may lag far behind. Who trains parents? The answer is, parents have been trained by their parents. How many times have you started a correction of your child only to realize, "I can't believe I sound like my parents."

Past Methods of Discipline Are Summed up by One of Three Methods

In each method, the focus was on treating the *symptoms* of the unwanted behavior while ignoring the *disease*—the reason behind what caused the unwanted behavior. The focus of past styles of discipline was to eliminate the negative behavior, usually with punishment and often without looking into why the behavior had occurred in the first place. These methods can be characterized in one of three ways:

1. Love withdrawal
2. Guilt induction
3. Power assertion

Love Withdrawal

Love withdrawal is the most subtle and yet most damaging of the three styles. It takes the form of the parent ignoring the child without giving a reason for the withdrawal. The parent attempts to control by acting cold or letting the child know by his silence and rejection how hurt and disappointed he feels by the child's behavior. While love withdrawal is used as a form of punishment intended to teach a child a lesson, if it happens for a long period of time and on a consistent basis, it can have a far-reaching and long-lasting negative impact on a child.

The child is not a miniature adult. Because of the subtlety of love withdrawal and lack of direct communication, it is difficult for a child to understand. The child feels punished but often does not know why he is being treated as he is. Parents who are thinking of their children as miniature adults capable of reading and understanding another adult's mind employ this tactic sometimes as a type of punishment. As a result, the parent judges the child for his failing and holds the child to a standard he might hold a more mature person.

The ultimate goal of this form of discipline is to leave the victim begging for forgiveness even though the child is not sure what he has done wrong. He is left with expressing "Whatever I did, I'm sorry I did it." The problems with this approach are numerous; it can cause children to suffer from depression, anxiety, and low self-esteem. While not appearing overly aggressive, the love withdrawal approach is strongly aggressive but masked behind a façade of passivity. Nothing is solved by silence. Until words are exchanged, healing cannot be set in motion.

In addition to the harm that love withdrawal inflicts on the child, the silent treatment also can have a very powerful boomerang effect. The child is learning a style that he can employ, at some future time, to get back at his parents and significant others in his life—a future spouse and even his own children.

Guilt Induction Can Be Very Effective in the Short Term
Guilt induction or *guilt tripping* is often not viewed as severe because children frequently need guilt. Without some guilt, there might be little or no obedience to social rules. However, when guilt induction is used as a primary disciplinary technique, the guilt inducer is frequently trying to engage in psychological manipulation and coercion. Sometimes the attempts are obvious and sometimes the attempts are not so clear. It is obvious with the parent who reminds the child of all the sacrifices he has made and how little appreciation he receives in return—"Can't you even pick up after yourself? Why are you always so lazy?"

Guilt induction can be used as an attempt to control by negatively comparing one child to another—"Why can't you be more like your brother? He does not have to be told over and over again." "Why is your room always a mess. You never seem to be able to do anything right." "Why can you not show any appreciation for all I do for you?"

Guilt induction can be very effective in the short term at achieving a desired behavior. However, the person on the receiving end eventually catches on to the process and frequently develops strong feelings of resentment toward the manipulator. Eventually, the person who is made to feel guilty may develop so much anger toward the person who is doing the manipulation that any guilt will be short-lived and only resentment will result.

Power Assertion Is Not a Good Long-Term Approach
Power assertion is perhaps the oldest and most used style of discipline because of its perceived efficiency. It is a strategy designed to gain compliance through coercion, pressure, forceful insistence, and a negative or critical interaction style. Essentially power assertion focuses on the negative behavior and aims at letting the child know who is boss. The parent demands conformity while imposing consequences for disruptive behavior. "Go to your room and stay there. You're grounded until I say you can come out!" While this approach may get results in the short term, all the data indicates it is not a good long-term approach. It is a strategy based upon punishment of the negative behavior and frequently creates a situation in which the level of punishment must be consistently increased with each new offense to get compliance. With an increase in the level of punishment comes the specter of bullying—an unacceptable consequence and possibly the beginning of another boomerang effect.

The Child Fights Back: What to Do?
What if the child refuses to obey his parent's orders? A potential problem in giving a direct order that must be obeyed, if

the parent is not careful, is that the child can quickly gain the upper hand by simply doing nothing. The child refuses; the parent becomes more and more frustrated. Which style of discipline does the parent adopt? With increased frustration, the parent is more likely to act out in an aggressive way. If this happens, remember whoever loses control; loses the battle—as in the public confrontation at the shopping mall described in Chapter 6.

In the face of a child's defiance, a shouting confrontation results in increased stress for the parent with accompanying anger and frustration. In the power assertion model, the frustrated parent must use more and more power. This is the beginning of the proverbial slippery slope and, if used, can take the situation to the edge of violence. Limits must and should be set to inhibit dangerous behavior.

Punishment by Itself Simply Will Not Work

Whatever the form of punishment chosen, punishment alone will not work for very long. Punishment may suppress behavior for a while but, as almost everyone would agree, it does not extinguish or eliminate negative behavior. Punishment may reduce the undesired behavior, but it is unlikely to eliminate the negative behavior completely. The really troubling part about punishment when used alone, is that the negative behavior comes back—usually more strongly than before the punishment was administered.

Does this mean that punishment in the form of limit setting should never be employed? No, it is not that simple. Punishment in conjunction with rewarding the desired behavior is quite effective. In fact, a combination of punishment and reward is the most effective way to change behavior.

Just what constitutes punishment in the form of limit setting? Limit setting can take many forms. For it to be effective, it does not have to be physical or even especially punitive. The child may see withholding the usual reward after a bad behavior as a punishment but it can be an effective way to get a child's attention and stop negative behavior. The effective paradigm is one of using a form of punishment and reward, summarized as *withhold reward from negative behavior while rewarding positive behavior.*

Choose a Punishment Wisely: Punishment Has a Purpose

Punishment should be used to arrest negative behavior and to get the child's attention so that the real work of change can begin. Suppose you decide to punish your child by grounding him. Will grounding in and of itself work to change behavior? Or are you using grounding as a way to address the underlying problem behavior and get your child to think about changing his negative behavior? If it is just about punishment, you have to be careful not to punish yourself at the same time. Suppose you decide that your child cannot go out on the weekend and you order him to stay home and study. You are going to have to enforce the punishment. So who is getting punished? Both you and your child!

One of the worst things a parent can do is to set a nonnegotiable punishment term—a sentence that must be served fully with no time off for good behavior. Once a nonnegotiable time of a punishment is instituted, there is the inevitable *unintended* consequence for which the parent is likely to pay.

Faced with a fixed-term punishment, the child serves out the punishment usually in an angry silence or with outright passive-aggressive behavior—acting out his anger by stomping around, slamming doors, deep sighs, or whatever else he can dream up to irritate the parent. When the sentence is completed, it is not over. The parent is left with an angry child with whom he will now have to deal.

The problem with the fixed-term punishment only oriented model is that it has the unintended consequence of punishing the parent as well as the child. Both lose. After all, if the child has to stay in to be punished, the parent also has to stay in to ensure the child is punished. *No one wins.*

It's a lose-lose situation. Now you are both trapped like the character Papillion, played by Steve McQueen in the classic film of the same name. In the film, the lead character, Papillion is sentenced for the commission of a crime to live in an isolated island prison. A warden is assigned to ensure no escape and to make life a little harder for the prisoners. At the beginning of the film, both Papillion and the warden look healthy enough but as the film goes on, the island takes its toll on both men. The point is they are both serving prison time on the same island. One might have a little more freedom but they are both stuck on the same island. By the end of the film, you are not sure who looks worse—the warden or the prisoner.

Behavior therapy has shown that punishment in and of itself may work in the short-term but does not work in the long run. In fact, the use of punishment by itself means that the undesired behavior will return—and, more than likely it will return stronger than it was prior to the punishment. The child, in effect, is saying, "You can't make me and, even if I do what you want, I'll get even with you later!"

One might ask, if punishment does not work, why do people continue to use it so much both in and out of the home? The answer lies in the fact that punishment often works at the beginning, when it is first imposed and when it is used in sufficient force to intimidate the offender. Punishment is attractive because when it works, it is speedy and makes the imposer of the punishment feel as though the child came out on top. The downside is that it makes the person who was punished angry, sometimes quite angry. Suppose you make the mistake of assigning a two-week grounding on a child and you are determined that the child should serve the entire punishment with no time off for good behavior or positive behavior.

Get Out of a Lose-Lose Situation: Offer to Negotiate

Whenever a sentence is fixed with no hope of lessening, both parties are going to lose. The child with nothing to gain or lose is now in the position to punish the parent for two weeks. The parent may feel as though he has fallen into the trap of not being able to go back on his word when, in fact, that may be exactly what needs to be done. What if the parent were to back down? If the parent were to say, "I think I was hasty in grounding you for two weeks. Let me think out loud about this for a moment." Will such a message really destroy parental authority going forward? Or, will the parent convey the idea that he can admit mistakes through being hasty—and is able to think things through and consider reaching a more just decision?

Use the 3 Strategies Approach

The parent can now proceed to present both points of view by *thinking out loud.* "I said you were grounded for two weeks but when I said it, I was speaking out of frustration. If I ground you for two weeks and not reconsider just because I said it— I'm not sure what that would accomplish. We all make mistakes when we resort to knee-jerk reactions. This is one of those times for me. Instead of grounding you for two weeks, let's say you are grounded for a week and, if you like, we can discuss what needs to be done to get past this. Don't you agree it would be better to negotiate rather than being grounded for two weeks?"

By doing this, the parent is admitting to doing something in a rash manner. And what is wrong with admitting a mistake? The only mistake you cannot recover from is the one you *think* you cannot recover from. After all, you want your child to admit when he makes a mistake. You are now modeling the behavior you would like your child to also demonstrate. You want your child to believe that if you make a mistake, you are willing to admit it, own it and do something about it. By thinking out loud, a parent diffuses a situation by placing both child and parent in a position to negotiate what must be done.

Give Your Child a Chance to Earn Time Off from the Back End of the Punishment

Instead of a nonnegotiable punishment term, suppose the parent was to set a sentence of being grounded for one week while offering the child the chance to earn time off from the back end of the punishment. As an example, it could be posed to the child: "If you would like to shorten the time you will be grounded, you might want to think of some positive behaviors that you could demonstrate that might earn you time off for good behavior at the back end of this week."

The parent is now looking for some positive behavior rather than staying focused on the punishment of the negative behavior. If the parent can think of some previous incident and describe it in a story format about how it was worked out, this can serve as a positive encouragement that negotiation and resolution are possible. The parent might say, " Remember when you had gotten some deficiencies from school last semester? You were late turning in assignments and were grounded for a couple of weeks until you caught up with your work? You really made an effort and showed daily improvement and were able to earn some time off from the back end of the two-week grounding period. You did a good job handling that accomplishment."

The parent then might say, "If we're going to negotiate the length of the punishment, it would probably be a good idea to first resolve the issue that started this problem. I will need to hear an apology for your behavior, and tell me what you will do for the future and tell me what positive behavior you will be willing to do to make up for the negative behavior."

Let the Child Make the First Offer: "What Are You Willing to Do?"

Once this phase of the apology is concluded, you can return your focus to reducing the punishment. You might say, "Let me hear your ideas about what you could do to show me you want to get this behind us and move on." If your child does not answer or waits for you to make the first offer, you would be wise not to do so, lest you bid against yourself. If you make the first offer and your child refuses because he thinks you are asking too much, the offer will likely be withdrawn.

Once again, the child should be invited to make an offer. If she doesn't, you should respond that that is perfectly all right. Encourage her to take her time and give it some thought. After a cooling-down period, a child is likely to see the benefit of negotiating. You may also employ the *Tell a Story* strategy at some point, suggesting that the situation has some similarity to films such as *Papillion*—except that in this case, the parent doesn't have to be on the scene for the entire time and can hire a babysitter to help supervise. The child now has the incentive to practice good behavior and negotiate with the parent. A win-win situation has now been set up.

3 Strategies Negotiation Introduces a New Paradigm for the Home

3 Strategies Negotiation is a method in which the parent builds upon a behavior management plan and may even appear to take a milder and gentler approach to giving directions. The child is involved in the process. Following the directions given by the parent highlights that the child is a cooperative individual. Not following a parental direction indicates that the child is not yet ready to take part. Remember, if your child is not yet ready you may have to make the water colder for a while.

The goal of this negotiation approach is to turn the interaction around in such a way that your child is essentially asking for conformity and change. In the midst of this negotiation, a parent can utilize a number of valuable tools: verbally reinforcing positive behavior, reframing statements of the child to create a new personal narrative, and using paradox in the face of rebellious behavior.

A positive negotiation is set up, as the difference lies not in the perception of one person winning by getting the upper hand (the parent) with the other person (the child) as a loser. Instead, both can win. Additionally, the effectiveness of consequences can be influenced by how they're viewed. The following are a few simple guidelines for:

Consequences—When Are Consequences Least and Most Effective?

Consequences are *least* effective when they:
1. Are viewed as a fixed sentence that must be served to the limit;
2. Are designed to close off negotiation;
3. Offer no alternative for a lessening of the sentence without negotiation.

Consequences are *most* effective when they:
1. Can be amended or lessened through positive, cooperative behavior;
2. Are designed to initiate dialogue rather than close it off;
3. Are used as a tool to achieve improvement through mutual beneficial negotiation.

Chapter 10 Questions

Am I still locked into an old style of discipline?

Am I avoiding the fixed sentence approach to disciplining?

Am I willing to let the child earn time off on the back end of the punishment for good behavior when I set limits on my child's behavior?

Chapter 11

YOUNGER CHILDREN AND EXECUTIVE DYSFUNCTION: THE USE OF THE 3 STRATEGIES APPROACH WITH YOUNGER CHILDREN

Billy is an active nine-year-old in the fourth grade. While he is generally considered to be a likable child, he is easily distracted by whatever is happening around him. If two other children are talking, Billy immediately stops whatever he is doing and tries to interact with them. When the teacher corrects Billy in an attempt to refocus him, it is only with great difficulty that Billy resumes the prior assigned task, as he wants to continue interacting with the other students.

Matthew, eight years old and in the third grade, quickly and exactly follows the rules of the classroom. He requires little in the way of correction during the school day. When Matthew is assigned to do a task, he is very cooperative and appears to try to do the best job he can as his teacher's approval is very important to him. Matthew follows directions and rules almost too extreme, often correcting other children when they deviate from what they should be doing. On days when the schedule deviates, Matthew becomes quite upset, to the degree of arguing with his teacher that the old schedule dictates he should be doing something else that he usually does at that time of day.

Both of these children appear to be different but both exhibit problems with executive function skills. Executive skills play a tremendous role in your child's development. A problem with the development of executive skills is so subtle that it has often been referred to as the *almost invisible disorder*. Despite its subtlety, it can have a profound effect on a wide variety of abilities and affect all aspects of one's life. The disorder is frequently overlooked and is often mistaken for laziness or carelessness.

The importance of developing good executive functions cannot be overemphasized. Executive skills cover a wide range of activities and form the basis for all future intelligent and goal-directed behavior. When these skills are present, the child develops smoothly while demonstrating the ability to initiate and stay focused throughout the process of learning and taking instructions. These are the children who keep their rooms neat, follow parental instruction, and adapt to new situations without undue stress. They experience success in college because they are able to apportion their time effectively; they make good decisions and focus on future goals that will help them choose productive careers.

The Scope of Executive Functions Is Wide

Executive skills cover a wide range of abilities including such things as:

1. Sustaining attention and concentration when working on projects;
2. Initiating work on projects that should be done for school;
3. Planning and prioritizing more complex projects requiring long-term commitment;
4. Organizing materials needed for projects in a neat and effective way;
5. Managing time effectively, sharing time between various projects.

These skills are incorporated into a useful inventory called the Behavioral Rating Inventory of Executive Functioning (BRIEF), which can be requested and filled out by parent and teacher to identify problems that may exist either in school or in the home.

In addition to these functions, there are behavioral indicators that are associated with properly functioning executive skills, including:

1. Response inhibition: the ability to inhibit responses such as calling out, interpreting other students or teacher.
2. Shift: the ability to stop one activity and move to another when directed.
3. Emotional control: the ability to react appropriately to setbacks and disappointments.

Warning Signs Indicating Problems with Executive Functioning Should Be Addressed

Studies on brain development show that the brain produces many more neural connections than it will ever need. By producing so many different connections, the brain has an inherent flexibility to learn from a wide variety of experiences. However, once the brain reaches maturity, the brain begins to rid itself of connections that have not been utilized in a process referred to as *pruning*. This getting rid of unutilized connections points to the importance of a child's early years.

If your child seems interested only in watching TV and playing video games or is doing poorly in school the problem may well lie with delay or failure to develop the skills that underlie these abilities. Individual problems may be part of a bigger dilemma of a failure to develop a whole series of fundamental skills referred to as executive functions. Your child may have difficulty keeping track of more than one thing at a time. He may struggle with telling stories, communicating details in an organized sequential manner, stopping one activity to begin a new meaningful activity. These are warning signs that indicate a problem with your child's executive functioning that should be addressed.

Planning and Prioritizing Activities Is Essential to Your Child's Development

A child should learn how to plan and prioritize activities, how to organize and manage time as well as demonstrate the persistence to follow through. If your child does not have the skills, it's no wonder you're constantly in a process of giving instructions and having them ignored.

A mental checklist to assess your child's development should include:

- When asked to begin a task, does your child start right away?
- Does your child exhibit good time management or poor time management?
- Does your child demonstrate goal-directed persistence?
- Is your child able to move from one task to another without upset or a temper tantrum?
- Is your child able to stop playing a video game when asked to do something else?

Numerous cognitive problems and emotional difficulties are often seen when executive skills fail to develop or are impeded by ADD, and/or a learning problem or significant learning differences. Before your child is labeled as rebellious and unwilling to cooperate, consider that he may not have developed executive skills to the point where he is able to take direction. Your child is probably not deliberately being inattentive—and raising your voice will certainly not work.

Problems created by failure of timely development of executive skills can be found in any number of situations. The child may not be able to begin a project or may begin a project but soon become distracted and fail to follow through. Whatever stage of the breakdown, it is likely to cause a great deal of frustration.

The first step in making any real progress with a child who is lacking important executive skills is to figure out the child's strengths and weaknesses. There are many good books on the topic of executive skills to help you understand these basic underlying functions and to help you learn to motivate your child in gaining executive skills. *Smart but Scattered* by Peg Dawson and Richard Guare is one such book.

Where to Begin?

Begin with defining the problem by assessing the situation. Where does the breakdown occur? If your child has difficulty getting started, task initiation should be the focus. If the child can promptly get started on a task but does not follow through, task persistence is the problem. Focus on and define the problem; put it into words. Remember, anytime we can put a problem into words, we have begun to find a solution. Conversely, if we cannot put the problem into words, we are not likely to find a solution.

Get Your Child to Ask for Help. Negotiate an Agreement. Use a Chart.

Because reward incentives are very helpful with younger children, they should play a large role at the outset. Remember, the younger the child, the greater the need for obvious positive reinforcement. Let's say the problem has to do with either beginning a new task in a timely fashion or following through once the task has begun.

Think out loud and define the problem for your child. "Let me think out loud about ways to improve how to keep you going once you begin to do something. You need to get better at how you stay with whatever you are doing longer until you complete what you start. Now, I could just tell you to do it and walk away— or I can work with you and help you. If I stay, we can talk things through and figure what we can do to move forward. Let's begin by setting up a chart to measure your improvement. That way, you can see your progress for yourself and at the same time, you can begin to earn rewards for your work."

The use of a timing device can be very helpful when dealing with tasks related to persistence. While you work with your child on persistence, begin timing your child. A chart is also a useful tool to promote change. Once your child stops working, show how long he was able to work and put a star on the chart titled "Staying on Task." You've now determined the baseline for task persistence. Every time your child works that long or longer, reward with another star. Do not attach a monetary value to a star.

You can now say, "You were able to work for two minutes and fifty seconds and you earned a star. Let's keep going so you can earn more stars. Do you think you can improve your performance?"

In future attempts blend in "asking" questions to lock in gains that your child is making while reminding him how well he did previously. "Remember the last time we tried this? You showed how well you could work when you put your mind to it. You are able to work on task for up to three minutes. Do you think you can do as well or better on this next try? Let's see how many stars you can earn this time. For every three minutes you are able to work, you can earn a star." You are now positively reinforcing your child's efforts with words of praise and with the visual stimuli of stars.

Let's suppose a worst-case scenario: You are having trouble engaging your child. Start the chart. Observe your child working on a task and when the child's persistence stops, put a star on the chart and say, "You earned a star because you were able to work for three minutes. If you can keep going like that, I am going to put more stars on the chart for you."

What Is the Value of Stars or Reinforcers?
Stars are worth whatever you say they are worth and their value can change from task to task. Actually, you are going to give rewards based on things that you are already doing for the child—things you usually give away for nothing—like making blueberry pancakes for breakfast or earning more time with a video game. To create a sense of earning something for effort, agree on the number of stars as a reward before the child begins the task or you

can wait until the next day to announce the reward. If you agree on the reward before beginning the task, you might say something like, "Okay, if you earn three stars, you will have earned blueberry pancakes for breakfast or time with your video game." If you did not agree on a reward before the child began the task, you can tell the child the next morning while serving blueberry pancakes for breakfast, "You earned blueberry pancakes because you worked so well on the task of following through."

There should always be a *price tag* to serve as an incentive. That price can be stated either before or after the task. If it is stated after the fact, there is always the chance to begin by asking questions. "Do you know why you were able to earn blueberry pancakes for breakfast? It is because you were able to work so well at the task we agreed to do and because you were able to follow through." It is important to reinforce the idea that rewards are earned. Be specific about the association between reward and behavior.

Now, you might be saying to yourself, "Well, that is okay but I've resolved only one small problem of a bigger problem." What you must realize is that by addressing one small problem, you are actually achieving much more. You are fostering the idea that your child can gain control over himself, and you are reminding your child that he is able to follow through on tasks and overcome challenges.

An Older Child's Understanding of Executive Skills Can Lead to Successful Negotiation

If your child is old enough to understand the importance of executive skills, you are in a better position to explain the purpose behind your work—and thinking out loud can play a larger role in successful negotiation. Begin by presenting both sides of the negotiation. "Let me think out loud about the importance of what we are trying to do. You may have other things you would rather do that are more fun, and I would agree with you that there are things you would rather be doing. On the other hand, this is a chance to learn some skills that will be important for your future. Your ability to persist with work—even when you do not want to do it—is important for you even though it might not make sense right now. I understand you want more time on the computer (video game or whatever), so I'm willing to negotiate with you for something each of us would like. Are you agreeable to negotiating?"

Each small success helps build your child's narrative, which you can use for all future challenges. "You are doing so well at staying with finishing what you start. You are showing me you are becoming more grown-up—that's what you need to do at school. I'm proud of your efforts, and I think you should be, too."

Get Your Child to Define the Steps to Success

Getting children out the door with all the things they need for the day is a frequent problem for parents. "Eat your breakfast. Comb your hair. Get your backpack on." Instead of issuing a series of last-minute directives, suppose you were to rehearse with your child the night before all the things that need to be done in the morning? Teach your child to verbalize the directions and complete the tasks. It is one thing for a parent to state the things that need to be done; it is quite another matter—and far more productive—if the child states the various things to be done with little or no prompting. Rehearsals provide the opportunity for a child to learn self-talk.

For a child who is trying to learn executive functioning, some tasks may seem overwhelming unless they are broken into smaller steps. It is the job of the parent to help make things less overwhelming. By learning how to identify the steps that are part of the overall task demands, your child will move away from a world of impulsivity and gain a sense of mastery over his world.

To succeed, your child will need a system of questions and answers that will serve as guideposts or objectives along the way. Let's look at an example. One of the more daunting tasks for a young child is to have to write a paper that requires utilizing a number of sources. You can begin by asking, "When is the assignment due?" When your child identifies the date, you can suggest, "Do you think it would be a good idea to put this on your calendar so you will know how much time you have?" When the child agrees to putting the date on the calendar, you can ask, "After you choose a topic, what do you think you need to do first? Identify the sources that you will use?" Follow up by asking your child to list the materials that need to be collected in order to complete the project. Help your child begin to identify the stages in the actual writing of the paper. A series of mini-timelines can be very useful and will avoid the last-minute panic as the due date draws near.

Parents Can Model Executive Skills

Parents can model executive skills by explaining to children how planners, organizers, or timers are used in the workplace or by showing how a vacation is planned. Let's say you have decided on a beach vacation and in an effort to have your children more involved, they are invited to help plan some of the activities. This can be done in a number of ways. Post activities on a board and give the children the task to prioritize the activities. Rainy-day activities can also be chosen and discussed to teach children how to shift from one activity to another depending upon weather conditions. Maps can be employed so that children can visually see how they are going to move from place to place. Packing for the trip can also be part of the planning activity. Ask, "What do you think you need to take along on the trip?"

Watch a Show that Incorporates Multiple Steps in the Production of a Product

Sometimes it is helpful to have a child watch an educational show. Tune to Discovery Channel's series *How Things Are Made* to get a sense of how complex tasks are comprised of a series of small individual steps. Films that demonstrate products being made are often fascinating for children. One episode about the making of chocolate chip cookies demonstrates the process of mixing the ingredients—white and brown sugar with butter before adding flour, baking soda, salt, and eggs. The episode follows forming the shapes through to the fast freezing before packaging. As you watch with your child, you can comment on the process as it is being described—how simple steps lead to a finished product. At the conclusion, you can reinforce how most projects are achieved by following a series of individual steps.

Create To-Do Lists for the Child
Create checklists and to-do lists to give your child a sense of time and how it should be managed. Show your child how you utilize time management planners and software to keep on schedule. The covert message that you will be delivering is that if you want to be seen as more adult, do the kind of things that adults do. Adults are organized, and adults do not need to be told what to do.

Sam: A Case Example
Sam had just turned seven years of age at the midpoint of first grade when he pushed another boy to the ground. This specific behavior was in the context of several other incidents in which he had become aggressive toward other children. He was evaluated using an IQ test and the Behavior Rating Inventory of Executive Function (BRIEF), which was completed by a parent and teacher.

Improvement was needed for *response inhibition* (the ability to think before one acts and to resist the urge to do something that may have a negative impact) and *emotional control* (the ability to manage emotions in order to achieve goals, complete task, or control and direct behavior). Both parent and teacher were in agreement with the need to improve these areas.

The immediate focus had to be on Sam's ability to interact with other children in more positive ways. Since the eighteen members of Sam's class sat in a circle, the first move was to create more separation by having children move a little farther apart. A behavior chart was introduced at school, a copy of which was sent home. This gave Sam's parents the opportunity to reinforce positive behavior the same as his teacher did.

The target goal defined for Sam was to figure out how to deal with another child who was seen as intruding into his space. Sam's parents and teacher were encouraged to think out loud when offering solutions as a way of modeling for Sam the behavior he was to employ, saying, "Let me think out loud about what I can do here." Then they began to outline possible alternatives.

Sam was encouraged to think out loud about possible solutions in a low, subvocal (quiet) voice. For example, when someone else was in his space, he could say to himself, "Let me see what I can do. I could push him away or I could walk away or I could tell the teacher what is happening and ask for help." Sam was also encouraged to make a list of things he could do when starting to get upset and record the times he was able to employ his adaptive strategies.

Sam showed good improvement for the rest of the year, and the next school year the new teacher reported continued growth and good ability to cope with new situations that might previously have been stressful.

Chapter 11 Questions

Am I focused on teaching executive skills?

Am I assessing what skills need to be defined and rewarded?

What value do I give to the stars that have been earned?

Chapter 12

CHARTING AND THE 3 STRATEGIES: WHY USE A CHART?

As was noted in the discussion of the adaptive unconscious in Chapter 5, all of us develop habituated behaviors over time consistent with the *adaptive unconscious*—behaviors that allow us to process information with minimal thinking. The adaptive unconscious makes us efficient since we do not have to spend a great deal of time thinking up novel ways to approach situations. Over time, we create a narrative about who we are, what we do, and what we like—making the habit patterns an integral part of ourselves.

When the choices that we make are positive as well as efficient, we have the best of both worlds. However, when the choices we make are negative, we are on the road to developing bad habits—habits that interfere with productivity and must be overcome. When there is a lack of agreement between parent and child, habituated behaviors often require a more systematic approach to determine if a problem does, in fact, exist and to ascertain its scope. Sometimes bad patterns of behavior can be cured quickly through focusing on the problem and suggesting alternative behaviors.

One of the struggles that currently affect many households has to do with abuse of the Internet. After trying a series of seemingly simple and straightforward solutions to problems associated with the Internet, we come to realize that despite the best intentions by all parties, progress toward the goal behavior is not being achieved because the child keeps slipping back into the problem behavior. It is at this juncture that greater awareness of the problem behavior is needed and a behavior chart should be considered. Regression to problem behavior after improvement can occur around many different types of issues. Internet and cell phone uses are both very addictive sources of problems, especially for teenagers, as well as for many adults.

The Scope of Internet Abuse Is Well-Documented

The American Academy of Pediatrics (AAP) has well documented the dangers of increasing availability of the media. Research by the AAP indicates that children are spending an average of seven hours a day on entertainment media, including televisions, computers, phones, and other electronic devices. These studies by AAP and many other studies have shown that excessive use of media can lead to a variety of issues including attention problems, school difficulties, sleep and eating disorders, and obesity. The Internet and cell phones also provide platforms for illicit and risky behaviors.

What constitutes Internet addiction? Several factors are important, including: a preoccupation and excessive use of time spent online; lying about or hiding from parents the actual time spent online; loss of interest in social activities outside the home; an inability to cut back on time spent online; and symptoms of irritability, anxiety and boredom when not online.

Because addiction is such an insidious process and because children—like adults—tend to hide an addiction in order to preserve it, the process of getting to the truth about your child's addiction may prove to be difficult. Faced with growing suspicion about your child's behavior—and in light of possible denial—you may need to begin tracking how much time your child is spending in front of the computer and introduce the behavioral chart.

Keep in mind that if your child is becoming addicted, he will be quite upset with any attempt to impose limitations. It is when the Internet seems to be used almost solely for recreation, that it can be problematic. This is where applying your negotiation skills is likely to be productive in helping your child understand his value system. You must attempt to maintain an open and respectful dialogue while being aware that your child may be quite frustrated at having to give up one his favorite pastimes.

Although you have valid concerns about exposure to inappropriate or harmful information, remember that the Internet can also be extremely beneficial. Often, the Internet is a necessary tool to complete school assignments and do on-line research. The fact that the Internet can be very advantageous should be weighted in when you supervise its use.

If your child is open to the monitoring of his Internet activity, there is likely little need for concern on your part. However, if he is displaying guardedness when using the Internet, it may be necessary for you to become more proactive with your supervision.

Begin by Thinking Out Loud When Introducing the Idea of a Behavior Chart

In introduction of the chart, it is important that the parent—in the spirit of negotiation—summarize both sides of opposing views in an evenhanded fashion. Begin by saying, "Let me think out loud about this. We need to determine how much time you are spending on the computer and if the time spent is consistent with the goals and objectives you say you value. You say you are using the Internet effectively within the time limit set. Time has a way of getting away from all of us. I am going to propose the use of a behavior chart so that we can be clear about how you are spending your time and how you must direct your efforts to goals that are important.

"A behavior chart helps you to keep track of your behavior. A behavior chart is just like my daily calendar—it tells me what I need to do each day, hour by hour. Now, I can understand that you may not want a behavior chart—and you may see it as a nuisance—but behavior charts like calendars are very useful. I'll tell you what, if you prove to me that you do not need the chart, we will discontinue it—but you must show me progress. The chart will help you do that.

"I want you to keep track of the time you spend on the Internet—how much time you are spending on studies compared to games and talking with friends. I don't mean to say I think you are deliberately doing things to abuse the privilege of Internet access. I do believe that a greater understanding about your use of the Internet will have some very beneficial effects for you. Keeping track of your behavior will improve your focus and keep you from wasting time. Again, I do not think you're doing anything wrong deliberately. I just want you to understand that I am trying to keep you from slipping into habits that will get in the way with your growth as a student and a person."

By thinking out loud, the child is liable to feel part of the negotiation process—although you've sent a clear message that the chart is nonnegotiable. If your child wants a life without a chart, he should be spending less time playing games and more time on productive activities. If this becomes the case, the ongoing use of a chart will not be necessary.

Behavior Management and Charting Behavior: Tell a Story to Overcome Objections

The switch to a behavior chart frequently draws an immediate objection from a child, and you may well have to deal with the disruption before proceeding. So, the question is, is the chart worth the upset it is likely to cause?

It is a principle of behavior modification that "charting behavior changes behavior." To get a sense of why charting changes behavior, it makes sense to go back to a famous study that was carried out at the Hawthorne Works, a division of Western Electric, in a factory outside Chicago. The study was conducted from 1924 to 1932 by the Harvard Business School to see if Hawthorne

Works could make its workers become more productive. Among some of the interventions attempted was one in which the levels of light were adjusted in various parts of the building. When the amount of light was increased, production went up—and when the amount of light was decreased in another part of the building, production went up. What's this? Production went up in both instances?

The workers' productivity improved when changes were made and slumped when the study was completed. It was concluded that the gain in productivity occurred due to the impact of the motivational effect on the workers as a result of the attention of being watched. Attention was identified as the important factor in improvement. The emerging principle that attention is the most powerful incentive has evolved into the rule that charting behavior changes behavior.

Ask Questions to Define Goals and Objectives

Fundamental to agreement between parent and child is the selection of more deeply rooted lifetime goals. Does the child want to succeed in school and learn study skills essential for future progress? Does the child want to go to college? While the answer to these questions seems obvious, getting the child to verbalize answers is vital.

Once the goals have been agreed upon, the objectives as to how to achieve the goals must be decided. If your child wants to get good grades, she must put in the necessary time. In helping her calculate the time needed to reach goals, the process revolves around asking questions and getting answers. Remember, it is important that questions are open-ended. Use of the "gotcha" question should absolutely be avoided. For example, you might say, "You have two hours open after school to spend on your schoolwork. How do you want to spread that time out over the number of subjects that you have to work on?" Answers to the questions should be written down and charted.

Children Resist Charting

Children resist the idea of charting for a number of reasons. The child realizes that the parent will become more aware of objectionable behavior and the amount of time being wasted on it. The child also knows that to follow the chart, his behavior will change. He will lose out on the more pleasant activity of playing games on the Internet or texting with friends. Faced with increased accountability, of course the smart child will object to charting.

Parents Are Also Resistant to Charting

If charting works, why is it, then, that so many of us are averse to doing it? We know it works and that it is used all the time—just ask Weight Watchers and other similar organizations. Charting works because it makes us aware of our own behavior. We pay more attention to ourselves and to what we are doing. When we look at our own behavior and do not like what we see, we are more likely to change. Despite the fact that charting behavior is effective, there is a resistance to using a chart for a variety of reasons. "It's too much work." "It's tedious." "I shouldn't have to do it." While all of these statements may be true, the fact is that charting behavior will work if the parent is willing to put the necessary effort into it.

Make the Child an Active Participant by Setting Limits and Charting Behavior

Many people are already familiar with the basic principles of behavior management. Point charts and incentives are accepted tools of intervention and, while they often seem tedious to use and are frequently viewed as too much trouble, they are effective.

A scoring system using points should be as simple as possible. Simplicity can be achieved by limiting goals to three behaviors at a time. A "yes" or "no" can be used to indicate whether the behavior has been achieved or not. Proper use of a behavior chart can help as a learning tool to transition to a more adult version—the Day-Planner. The chart may reflect:

1. When did the child log on and off the computer.
2. How much time was spent on a school-related goal.
3. How much time was spent on entertainment.

It is not just about counting points—it is about the negotiation of the chart that is equally as important as the chart. Using the three strategies (ask questions, tell stories and think out loud) makes the parent more than just a bookkeeper tabulating points and then distributing rewards. Your role as parent is to effect an interaction more appropriate to lasting change. Open avenues for parent/child negotiation of behavioral goals. Recognize that your child is far more likely to internalize the lesson learned from the process when he has been an active participant in defining it. Go back to the example of the Hawthorne Effect and recall how employees were positively affected when they realized that their behavior was being studied. It is important that your child feel observed.

Negotiation adds another constructive dimension. Negotiation introduces principles that allow the parent to maintain both authority and respect while not diminishing the feelings of value and self-worth critical to the child's self-esteem. Negotiation avoids the blame game and positions the parent in the role of interest and concern. In effect, the parent is saying, "These goals represent something that we both agreed to implement."

Charting Can Be Used for a Variety of Other Behaviors
A chart can make a difference with almost any behavior that it proves because it gives you a chance to interact, talk with, and negotiate a solution with your child. A chart can even be used to put the child in a position where he *wants* to negotiate. Let's suppose your child refuses to participate in selecting goals that are placed on the behavior chart. You can begin the chart without your child's participation by saying, "You are apparently not ready to participate in creating a behavior chart. That's fine;

I can start one without your participation and I will select the goals."

Review the chart at the end of the week and tell your child what rewards he has or has not earned. Encourage participation going forward but do not dole out punishment for a lack of involvement. If your child continues to demonstrate resistance to negotiating, encourage continued cooperation and leave the door open to future negotiation. Think of the chart as your child's calendar. We all use calendars. They allow us to plan. They keep us on schedule. They allow us to chart ourselves. Why not use it with the kids? If negotiation is needed:

1. Decide what behaviors should go on the chart.
2. Decide when and under what conditions the chart should be discontinued.
3. Decide under what conditions the chart should be restarted.

What Is the Fundamental Goal of the Behavior Chart?
Before you say, "Oh no, not that. I hate behavior charts. They're too much work," know that a chart can be used in a less painful way than you may have used it before.

Behavior charts must always be stated positively—never negatively. The chart should always reflect the behavior you want— never the behavior you want to discourage. If you want someone to walk, you say, "Walk." You should not say, "Do not run." (If you use the word *run* in the directive, the other person will hear *run* and probably start running.)

Suppose the chart were to read, "Do not fight with your sibs." Whether the answer is a yes or no, the word *fight* is emphasized and the absence of negative is not necessarily positive. Instead, suppose the chart were to read, "Play and speak politely to your siblings."

The child either gets a check mark next to this goal or the space is left blank. That way, you can tell at a glance whether your child is doing well. If your child is doing well, reward with praise: "You did a good job!" If there are very few check marks or stars, encourage your child to improve. "What do you think you can do to earn more checkmarks?" Avoid saying negative things, which will only earn you a negative reaction: "All you do is criticize me."

Choose the Goals and State Them in a Positive Form

In selecting the goals to be achieved, look at the behaviors that you do not want and then write them in a positive form. If you want someone to speak in a polite tone of voice, the goal should be written as "Speak in a polite tone of voice." Do not write, "Do not yell." There should be *no more than three goals* on the chart at any point in time. More than three goals can look overwhelming and produce an immediate rejection of the chart. Once one behavior goal seems to have been mastered, a new goal can be suggested as a substitute.

Negative Goals and the "Dead Man Rule"

It is worth repeating: There should be no negative behaviors stated in the chart. Any statement of a negative behavior fails the "Dead Man Rule." What, you may ask, is the Dead Man Rule? The Dead Man Rule states that you should never ask anybody to do anything if a dead man can do it better. If your direction is "Do not shout," a dead man will succeed 100 percent of the time. If a dead man can do it better, do not include it in a behavior chart. Only put positive behaviors on a chart. If you want the child to speak in a normal tone of voice, write the goal as "Speak in a normal tone of voice."

When your child has successfully completed assigned behaviors for an agreed-upon period of time, he will likely ask what the reward is. Parry this request by asking what your child wants. Remember, the parent never starts the bidding. If you do, you will be bidding against yourself. Just because your child states what he wants, doesn't mean that it has been earned. Respond with something like, "Yes, you have done much better, but I do not think you've earned all of that yet… maybe just some of it."

Suppose You Decide to Use Points Instead of a Simple "Yes" or "No"

With a standard behavior management approach, the goals and methods of the program are parent-selected. If the child performs at or meets the criteria established by the program, the child receives points or incentives. If the child refuses to comply, points are not awarded. *Points are never taken away* after they have been earned. Once the current issue is resolved, points can be used later. The purpose about not taking away points is very important. Taking something away from someone who believes it belongs to him creates an immediate hostile response.

Imagine yourself sitting in a classroom with a speaker who offers to put a dollar down in front of you if you pay attention. As soon as a few dollars are distributed, everyone's attention becomes more and more focused. On the other hand, imagine if the speaker tells everyone to put a dollar on top of his desk and, if in the speaker's judgment, you are not paying attention, the speaker will take your dollar away. If someone takes your dollar away, trouble—or at least an argument—will ensue. You probably would be reluctant to put the dollar on the desk to begin with and you most certainly would object if the speaker were to take your dollar away.

What Are Points Worth?

It's important to not assign a dollar amount to points. Points can be used any way the parent wants. One of the best ways to use points is to allow your child to trade points for things of non-monetary value like freedom (going out with friends) or use of a computer and/or video game.

Trading points gives you an opportunity to negotiate with your child. If your child wants something bad enough, he will be willing to negotiate for it. You do not have to come up with a special reward. Try letting the child earn some of the things you have been giving away for nothing. If you do not put a value on something, what is it worth? The answer is…*nothing.*

Behavior management is a powerful process for a variety of reasons:

1. It charts behavior, allowing the behavior in question to be viewed as a process toward a goal—as such, it enables an examination of progress. It makes both the parent and child aware of what needs to be done, in specific terms that are observable and measurable.

    The system works at its most fundamental level because it gives attention to the behaviors that one wants to incentivize. Since attention is the single-most powerful reinforcer, behavior changes.

2. It rewards conformity and produces pressure to "get with the program." It does this most efficiently when a nonconforming child sees other children—in the case of siblings or members of a class at school—getting rewards while they are not. Because children understand they can likewise be rewarded, the pressure mounts to conform. Peer pressure is thus applied for positive goals.

When Should the Chart Be Discontinued?

Simply put, the answer is when it is no longer needed. When the behavior chart seems to be a way of confirming that things have improved to the degree where the chart is no longer needed, the parent can suggest that the chart be discontinued. Usually, the child is just as eager to discontinue the chart.

You can say something like, "I think we can agree that the chart is not really necessary at this point in time. However, it has worked well for us and we can begin it again if we need to do so. You can either tell me you want to continue the chart or show me by your behavior that the chart is not needed. I will listen to your words and your behavior but I will always pay special attention to your behavior."

Chapter 12 Questions

When charting behavior:

Am I making the child an active participant in the process?

Am I limiting the chart to as few behaviors as possible (a maximum of three)?

Are the behaviors on the chart stated positively (avoiding the "Dead Man Rule" trap)?

Am I handling the points to be earned effectively?

When should I consider discontinuing the chart?

Chapter 13

THE RESISTANT CHILD: DESIGNING AND CHARTING A PROGRAM

When you give a direction, it is expected that your child will comply. When he is resistant, the first question that must be answered is what is he hoping to achieve? Is he just asserting himself and refusing to be told what to do? Or is something else at play here?

When dealing with a resistant child, it is important for you as a parent to understand at the outset what the motivation is behind the resistance. Sometimes the answer is as simple as your child prefers to have fun rather than do work. Sometimes, the problem is more complicated. What if there is a more dangerous pattern of behavior and your child's resistance is contrary to the very nature of everything you want to instill? What if you find an empty bottle of liquor or drug paraphernalia in your child's room? How serious a problem are you facing?

An Example of Teenage Resistance

Chris is a bright young man and currently a high school senior. Generally, he is polite and appears to follow instructions given by his parents. Chris is viewed as a good student and liked by many of his teachers. His relationship with his friends, however, is quite another story. Chris most often feels socially lost and unaccepted when he is among his peers. He tries to gain acceptance by sitting with some of the popular kids in the cafeteria. Chris feels his "differentness" most severely when he hears other kids making weekend plans. He keeps hoping he will be invited to one of their many parties. On those few occasions when he is invited to (parentally unsupervised) parties, he makes the usual teenager excuses to his parents about where he was going. Thinking it will help make him part of the in-crowd, Chris does some drinking. He is able to hide the parties and his drinking from his parents by saying that he was staying over at friends' houses for sleepovers. Being able to fly under the radar emboldens Chris to attend other unchaperoned get-togethers where drinking is the rule.

Still, Chris does not feel part of the in-group. Opportunity presents itself—he sees a chance to gain attention and acceptance from his lunchtime friends! Chris's parents will be out of state Friday until Sunday attending a family function. He impulsively invites five young men at his lunch table to come over to his house for a party.

As is typical in this situation, the invited kids spread the word and invite a few more friends. A couple of the boys bring beer, hard liquor, and pot. Before long, the number of kids at the party swells to between twenty-five and thirty. Chris panics at the thought that his parents will find out. He fears things will be broken in the house or that one of the neighbors might call the police at the sight of all the parked cars and the noise level. With difficulty, he manages to shut down the party. After Chris gets his friends out of the house, he looks at the mess they left behind and his level of panic increases. Chris starts cleaning in an attempt to cover up the evidence.

Chris debates his options. *What should I do? Should I tell my parents about inviting a few friends over and describe what happened—or not?* Since he has time to clean up the house, Chris decides to try to keep the party a secret from his parents.

When Chris's parents arrive home on Sunday, they do not seem to notice any difference in the house. Still, it takes a couple days until Chris begins to breathe a sigh of relief that he got away with having a party against his parents express wishes.

Just before the weekend, Chris's parents confront him. They want to know what happened while they were away. They get out in front with Chris on their questions by telling him, in a frank manner, what they have learned from the neighbors, and they ask Chris why he disobeyed their directions. He explains he intended only to have a couple of friends over and that it was his friends who invited the others. Chris is asked if alcohol and drugs were involved. With suspicions aroused, Chris's parents ask about previous events—movies outings and overnight sleepovers. Chris is asked if this is the first time he has lied about his activities.

Chris, afraid that he will not be able to attend future parties, denies wrongdoing. Not buying what Chris is selling, his parents begin calling other parents and discover that Chris has lied to them about attending parties. Infuriated by his lying, Chris's parents are initially at a loss as to what to do. Again, they decide to confront Chris in a face-to-face exchange, citing what they have discovered.

Confrontations Can Be Good: The Confrontation with Chris
While the word *confrontation* frequently has a very negative connotation, confrontations can be very effective if the rules are understood and applied correctly. A good confrontation confronts the behavior, not the person. The positive confrontation is most certainly *not* about parents lecturing a child about what a bad person he is and how they cannot trust him in the future. Rather, the parent confronts the child's words and behavior as inconsistent, without attacking the child as a person. A positive confrontation does not judge or demean the person—rather, it focuses on what the child has said and what the child has done. It places the conflict inside the child—it is the child's task to resolve any apparent contradiction between his words and his behavior.

To achieve a successful outcome, a parent should make minimal use of the classic *I versus you*—as in, "I told you I did not want you to attend any parties where the parents were not home. How could you have done that?" Instead, a parent should rely upon the *you versus you* exchange—as in, "You told me you were going to a friend's house to watch a movie and instead you went to a party. Why did you tell me one thing and do another?" Utilizing this technique, the parent is challenging the child's words—and how his words do not match his behavior. Essentially, the parent is saying, "I don't understand why you would tell me one thing and do another? Can you explain this for me?" There are no angry exchanges, and no threats or lectures. The parent asks questions and waits for answers. By confronting the child in this manner, the parent places the conflict inside the child and waits for an explanation. The parents need to relax, take a breath, and remember that nothing has to be decided right away and that time is on their side.

Chris, faced with the evidence that other parents have enlightened his parents, admits to lying. At the time of confrontation, however he is unable or unwilling to talk. Chris's parents tell him to take his time and think things through and that when he is ready to discuss the matter with them, they will listen.

When Chris finally approaches his parents, he expressed how he views attending parties as a way to make friends. Chris's defense for his behavior is to tell his parents how miserable and friendless he feels. Chris believed he had to go to the parties or he would have felt even more isolated going forward. Chris persists—he wanted to continue to go to parties but promises that he will not drink or do drugs. His parents ask him how safe he feels attending parties where there is no parent at the home. Then they ask him a series of questions: Does going to a party without their permission outweigh the lack of credibility he has going forward? They wonder aloud how Chris could give his word so easily and not honor it.

Despite their upset with his behavior, Chris's parents are able to sympathize with his feelings. They want him to have friends but are afraid that he does not see the risk in his behavior. The parents are aware from reading newspaper articles and from hearing from other parents that there is a whole network of kids planning weekend parties when parents are away. Of paramount importance, Chris's parents want him to be safe. They want to believe their son's word that he will not drink or do drugs if he attends a party. Faced with their anxiety and their son's resistance to explain his values, Chris's parents are advised to try to get Chris to write a structured narrative about his experience. They want Chris to clarify his goals and values and to express them in his personal narrative.

What Is Writing As a Therapeutic Technique?

James Pennebaker, a University of Texas psychologist, developed a therapeutic approach based on story writing. In his book, *Opening Up* and *Writing to Heal,* Dr. Pennebaker set forth the basic principles of therapeutic writing. He assigned students the task of writing about their deepest emotions and emotional upheaval that has been influencing their lives. The assignment was to take place over four days, with the students writing continuously for twenty minutes a day. He told the students that spelling, grammar, and punctuation were not important, as this was not meant to be a literary assignment. Instead, the students were to focus on the story itself. The students were further instructed to tie this significant experience to their childhood, relationship with parents, people they have loved or love now—or even their career.

Research studies on the work of Dr. Pennebaker show that writing therapy has proved to be very effective in a variety of situations. Dr. Pennebaker's approach was modified in this case to having Chris write about his behavior toward his peers and to self-examine how his behavior was consistent or inconsistent with his goals and values in life. How does Chris want to be seen by others? By his parents? By his peers? Does he want to be known as a person of integrity—or someone who would say anything in order to be able to do whatever he wanted? This approach is a variation of the theme of the 3 Strategies Approach: Ask

Questions, Think Out Loud, and Tell Stories. In this instance, it is Chris who is to *tell the story*. It is to be Chris's story—a story about him, told by him.

Writing therapy appears to work because it allows the person to step back and assess his behavior in the context of the principles that will guide his life. As a rule, people do not believe something because someone else is saying it; rather, they believe something because they hear themselves saying it. It is one thing to mislead a person by omission when engaged in conversation. However, it is quite another matter and more difficult to mislead when using the written word. The written word can be examined in a variety of ways. Is it consistent throughout? Is it truthful—or is the writer holding something back?

Four days later, after completing the assignment, Chris's parents met with him again. This meeting gave the parents a good chance to better understand their son's behavior and to give him their reflections about what he had written. Chris's parents were impressed by the thoughtfulness of his writing and how Chris appeared to have come to an understanding of the need to preserve his truthfulness although it might cost him loss of friends in the short term.

Even though we may be emotional creatures 90 percent of the time—when we do pause and think about what has happened to us and where we are going—our minds are designed to try to understand, process and make our experiences part of our personal narrative. When experiences are put into language, situations are created that allow individuals to begin to solve difficulties. It is a principle that whatever can be put into language, can be solved and whatever cannot be verbalized, remains an unsolvable puzzle.

Chris's parents have an invaluable tool in his writing. They are able to go back over their son's writing and ask questions, share experiences with him, and offer praise for his work. Chris can be reminded through his own words that he can put a negative experience behind him and move forward.

But What If Chris Refuses to Write?

Smart children often see specific outcomes and consequences of their behaviors. Chris may be thinking that if he does this writing, he may wind up holding himself to a standard that he is not interested in upholding. As a result, Chris may object, saying the writing exercise is silly or stupid. He may ask, "Why can't I just say what I will do? Why do I have to write it?" Or Chris may complain that he does not have time to spend twenty minutes a day for four days to engage in a ridiculous exercise.

It should be pointed out to Chris that he needs to rearrange his schedule to find the time. He can be reminded that he needs to spend twenty minutes less time texting friends or playing games on the computer. If Chris still refuses, he can be asked if he wants to do the work in his room or would he rather work at the dining room table after dinner. The message to Chris is unmistakable: It is not a question of whether he will do the writing assignment or not. It is a question of when he will do it. Since it is in Chris's best interest to get the *punishment* behind him, it is likely that he will start sooner than later.

What About Writing Therapy for Younger, Resistant Children?

The process described above with Chris may or may not be as effective with younger children for a variety of reasons—and it may not be needed. However, writing about a problem might be a good habit for a child to begin to develop for the future. Younger children may not be able to work at writing for twenty minutes. Younger children may not understand what is meant by goals and values. If this is the case, the writing therapy can be reduced considerably to five or ten minutes for three days. Writing therapy is not a stand-alone approach. With the younger child, the interaction between parent and child is even more critical. The parent must be sure that the child understands and appears willing to incorporate what has been written into future behavior. In addition, the systematic reward method is most likely to be needed to overcome resistance.

Earning Rewards to Overcome Resistance Is Effective

Every successful reward system starts with identifying the problem behavior and its causes. Once the problem behavior is identified, competing and more positive behavior must be substituted. Resistance to changing behavior usually means the child is finding the negative behavior more rewarding than the work that should be done. It should be kept in mind that negative behavior is *not bad in and of itself.* There is nothing wrong with taking a break from homework, texting friends, or going online. Rather, it is the productive behaviors that suffer as a result of the amount of time the child is spending unproductively.

One advantage that you have as a parent is that your child has already told, with her behavior, the rewards that are likely to be effective: for instance, the importance of the cell phone and the computer. When a parent is faced with a child's resistance to effect a change, the child's desired behavior should be treated as a reward to be earned. In the future, the time spent on texting and use of the computer, should be earned by successfully completing homework and chores.

Reward Is Important and Should Be Earned

Rewards are important and should be earned, although children often object to having to earn what they think is their right—something they should be getting for nothing. This is true for both children and adults. We know that an adult applying for a job will have as a top question, "What does the job pay?" It is the reward that will be earned in exchange for the work. Even if the job applicant does not ask the question about salary, you can bet it is on the mind of both parties.

Be Prepared to Identify Alternative Behaviors

A parent must be prepared to help the child find alternative rewards. Make it clear that you want your child to socialize with other children. Encourage visits at others' houses as long as there is an adult present. Likewise, invite your child to have friends over. School-sponsored activities are also a great way for children to be able to socialize. There are any number of outdoor activities like swimming, tennis, skiing and cycling that engage children both mentally and physically and can be encouraged by parents. The child may be able to earn rewards by successfully doing physical outdoor activities. It is important to create habits that will make your child feel healthy and that will carry on into adulthood.

External Rewards Are the Way the World Works
External rewards are important because, quite simply, that is the way the world works. As a parent, it is your job to teach your child the perception of the world, as you know it. Even though it is the way the world operates, parents frequently give things away for nothing. Parents tend to see rewarding behavior as using bribes to get their children to do what they should be expected to do. Many parents object to rewarding positive behavior. Many have said, "I'm not going to bribe my child to do what is right." Or a parent may be holding to the principle, "I want my child to work because it's the right thing to do."

In a perfect world, it would be great if everyone could internalize goals and values without having to be rewarded externally—but this is a process that must be learned. As a child grows older and his mind develops, perhaps he will learn to internalize values. However, if a child is having a problem with lack of focus and wasting too much time, just hoping the child will develop a value system without rewards is unrealistic and unlikely. Rewards are effective and efficient to shape behavior in the present. Children, as they mature, may eventually develop good principles to live by without using rewards as an incentive.

Always introduce ideas by implicitly saying, "This is the way the world works. Work diligently, do what you're supposed to do and you will be rewarded." Think of the rewards you offer as you would a salary. Adults in the working world get paid for working. A salary is something one gets for doing what one is supposed to do. *Earnings* for work are not the acceptance of a bribe. A bribe is something used to get someone to do something that is wrong.

The Negotiation Process Begins with Each Party Wanting Something

As long as your child wants something, you have the beginnings of a negotiation. If your child wants nothing, then it is quite likely that you may have given away too much too easily. If this is the case, your child may well be thinking, "I should not have to work for what I am entitled to have." Never having had to work for anything is the child's basis for resistance.

Bringing the Child to the Negotiation Table Is a Means of Maximizing the Child's Focus

Bringing the child to the negotiation table may call for initial decisive action on the part of the parent. It may require you to cut back or possibly cut off some of the things that the child has been receiving for nothing. It should be noted that this approach is not intended as a punishment but rather as a means to get the child's attention to focus on what needs correcting. In selecting incentives that will maximize your child's resolve to improve or rectify situations, you need look no further than to see what your child chooses to do with his time on a day-to-day basis. If your child is spending three or four hours a day on the computer or cell phone, that is what is important to him. State what is needed from your child and determine and negotiate what your child is willing to do to earn rewards.

Use of Time to Overcome Resistance: Get on the Child's Meter

Time can become an important element in the reinforcement process. Unless there is interaction between child and parent, there can be no resolution.

Let's assume your child wants to play sports or engage in some other activity after school. The pressure is on him—not on you—to get to the activity (unless you decide to take that pressure upon yourself). Since your child must get to the activity sooner than later, the likelihood that your child will want to quickly resolve an issue is increased. Your child will not want it to stand in the way of attending the activity. Hopefully, a careful resolution of the matter will also increase the child's resolve to avoid similar problems in the future.

You have succeeded in making the point that there is only one thing stopping your child from enjoying a privilege and that is his behavior. The knowledge that you are in charge maximizes the pressure on him to resolve the disagreement. Once your child cooperates by participating in the resolution process, the incentive (reinforcer) is there for him to enjoy. The child's knowledge that he is in charge of beginning and ending the standoff maximizes the pressure he feels to resolve the issue sooner rather than later. There is absolutely no advantage in going back to the old Power Assertion model, the one in which the parent attempts to use physical force to get the child to go to his room. The whole idea of physical force is foolish and unacceptable. Even if the parent can physically drag a child to his room, keeping him there is another situation entirely.

Suppose instead of dragging the child to his room, the parent uses paradox and says, "Okay, take your time and go to your room when you want. But just know this: For every minute that it takes you to begin your time-out, you will owe me that time when you're ready to come down and talk to me about the behavior that resulted in you having to go to your room."

As discussed in Chapter 8, this process appears to put the child in the driver's seat. However, the child is only in the driver's seat in so far as he can begin the punishment and therefore have a voice in ending the punishment. This type of encounter causes the child to internalize ("Start or stop, it's up to me.") rather than externalize the conflict (the parent and child staring defiantly at each other). The child is no longer in a position of power because he cannot continue the rebellion by simply being quiet or not conforming. By having to speak to end the stalemate, the child who thinks he is in the driver's seat actually loses power and must give the parent what is being asked—or the punishment could last a long time.

Chapter 13 Questions

Am I focusing on behavior rather than the child?

Am I selecting the right incentives?

Can I use writing therapy to effect change?

Am I tying privileges to cooperative behavior?

Am I using time as a way of getting my child to negotiate sooner than later?

Chapter 14

CONFIRMATION BIAS AND

RESISTANCE TO CHANGE

A number of years ago, a mother brought her seven-year-old boy, Tommy, to my office. She was concerned. Her son seemed unhappy and depressed, frequently crying because he believed he did not have any friends. Tommy was able to verbalize the difficulties he was experiencing. Tommy would go to the schoolyard during recess with his classmates but instead of interacting with them, he would merely stand around because no one invited him to play. Tommy portrayed his classmates as ignoring him and not wanting to talk with him. I asked him questions: "How long has this been happening?" and "What happens when you ask the other children if they will play with you?" Tommy said he had not asked the other children because he was afraid they would say no. Tommy also interpreted his classmates' behavior as unfriendly and rejecting—"They don't like me." Tommy's mind was already made up. He would read their behaviors as rejecting. When Tommy was encouraged to be more direct about wanting to join games and to ask if he could play with his classmates, he reiterated that he was sure he would be rejected.

I told Tommy a story about how people in other countries train baby elephants when they reach a certain age to stay safe and not run away. A young elephant is separated from the herd and a rope tied around the bottom of its leg, which is attached to a spike that is driven into the ground. The young elephant tries to pull away from the rope to rejoin the herd but it is not able to do so because the elephant is not strong enough yet to pull the stake out of the ground. After attempting to get away for several days, the elephant stops trying. As time goes by and the elephant grows bigger and stronger, it could pull the stake out of the ground with apparently little effort and walk away but the elephant does not do so. "Why do you think the elephant does not try to escape?" I asked. Tommy replied that the elephant is not aware that it can get away. "Are you like the young elephant in the story that does not think it can succeed and does not try anymore? What do you think would happen if you asked the other children if you could play with them?"

"They might say yes." Tommy said. "That's right," I answered. "The elephant would probably succeed but is trained to think that it cannot get away and so it has quit trying." Tommy's eyes brightened as he realized—even if he could not understand the principle of *cognitive bias*—he was a victim of his bias and that was what was holding him back. The question for Tommy was one of taking a risk and asking for what he wanted. He began to understand. The following day, Tommy went to the playground during recess and asked the children if he could join them in play. He was immediately accepted and reported back to me the following week about his success.

What Is Confirmation Bias and How Does It Work?

People, in general, gather information in a very selective fashion. Confirmation bias is a tendency among people to focus on and pay attention to information that confirms a preconceived belief. People display bias in their everyday lives in the choices they make, the articles they read, and in the news programs they watch. Liberals tend to read articles written by liberals; conservatives tend to read articles written by conservatives. Confirmation bias interprets more ambiguous evidence in such a way as to support an individual's existing beliefs. It's not about people being stubborn and consciously ignoring information, it is an efficient automatic process—it is how our brains work.

Confirmation bias was at work in Tommy's brain. It gathered information that proved (albeit falsely) that it was futile to ask other children to play with him.

Confirmation bias works well for us because we have to process a tremendous amount of information on a daily basis. Just like the adaptive unconscious makes for efficiency, confirmation bias allows us to come to conclusions in a very efficient (although sometimes) somewhat skewed way. If we pay attention only to information that confirms what we already know, we do not learn anything new and have much less information to process.

A Stanford University Study Relevant to Confirmation Bias

In 1979, researchers at Stanford studied how confirmation bias affects the way people interpret new information. The study consisted of forty-eight subjects who either supported or opposed capital punishment. The participants were presented with two studies on capital punishment. One study appeared to confirm—and the other seemingly disconfirmed—the participants' existing beliefs about the ability of the death penalty to deter crime.

Both of the studies were created by the researchers and designed to influence the subjects in one direction or the other. After the subjects read the materials, they were asked if their opinions had changed and how convincing was the research they had been given in influencing their opinions. Almost all reported their initial belief remained unchanged. They noted details in the study that supported their opinion and ignored evidence that contradicted their opinion. The subjects listed studies that supported their preexisting point of view as superior to those that contradicted their initial point of view. They elaborated by listing specific ways in which the study they agreed with was superior to the other study. Clearly, they were confirming their own preexisting biases. (An excellent review of cognitive bias can be found in an article by Raymond S. Nickerson, "Confirmation Bias: A Ubiquitous Phenomenon in Many Guises, Review of General Psychology," 1998, Vol. 2, No. 2, 175-220)

Studies also show that if people gather and interpret evidence in a neutral manner, they may still remember it selectively to reinforce their expectations. This phenomenon is referred to as selective recall or confirmatory memory. Why does this happen? There is no clear-cut answer. One theory states that information consistent with prior beliefs is easier to store and recall than information to which we do not agree. Whatever the reasons underlying biased memory, it seems to exist as part of our overall confirmation bias.

Confirmation Bias—Shaping Your Child's Values: The Media, Peers and Parents

There is little doubt that many forms of the media are significantly influencing members of today's world, whether it is through television, music, or the Internet. Advertisers use the media to promote how people should dress, what they should eat, and what values they should hold. Just as the impact of television in the 1950s influenced American households, the Internet has taken a prominent place in today's society. Various estimates show preschool children watch nearly three and a half hours of TV per day—and this average continues through age eighteen. Despite the impact of television, increased use of computer games and the Internet seem to be overshadowing the watching of TV. Going forward, there are advantages and disadvantages as we continue to adapt to new technologies and social media. One thing is certain: Just as television has become part of our everyday lives—new technologies will continue, on an ongoing basis, to influence the way we live.

Critics have come forward to warn of the increased use and misuse of the Internet and cell phones by children. Many researchers are questioning the effects on children who spend excessive amounts of time using technology—especially on social networking websites and using cell phone text messaging programs. There is great concern that the use of social media does not increase social skills; rather, it makes children less social. Critics point to examples of children attending social events who engage in texting rather than speaking to the people who are present. Because the use of social media has increased so dramatically in recent years, it is important for parents to be aware of social media sites and to determine what effect these sites are having on their children.

Use of Social Media Presents an Opportunity for Parents and Children to Negotiate

Unquestionably, there are many positive uses for social media. It allows children to connect on group homework projects, and it allows them to exchange ideas regarding various social and educational activities. Because of social media's potential positive uses, parents need to keep an open mind before focusing on possible negative effects. The use of the Internet and cell phones is another opportunity for parents to discuss with their children how they are using the media and how it is influencing their core values. If a child is spending excessive amounts of time gaming on the Internet or has difficulty getting through meals without frequent texting interruptions, the behavior needs to be examined and action should be considered. Rather than just coming down on the child by unilaterally restricting Internet behavior and ordering change, a parent could seize the chance to modify behavior through the process of negotiation.

How Does a Parent Handle His Child's Cognitive Bias?

Attacking someone's cognitive bias directly is almost sure to be doomed to failure. The more we argue against a person's belief in an effort to change his mind, the more he will defend the belief and adhere to it. Cognitive bias has to be approached more indirectly by *adding additional information* that broadens the scope of one's point of view. To do this, the parent must be willing to listen to the child's point of view and be able to repeat back what he has heard. In repeating back the child's point of view, it is important for the parent to try to present that point of view as well or even more completely than the child presented it.

Barry is a 16-year-old, above average, high school student just starting his junior year of high school. He is generally conscientious about his schoolwork as he has college aspirations. However, his current academic year has gotten off to a difficult beginning as a result of an illness that caused him to miss several school days. Barry is now behind on a number of papers that are coming due. In addition, he is preparing for SATs.

Barry approaches his parents to ask if he can attend a Thursday night concert over an hour's drive from home. His parents have a general rule about no concerts during the week but Barry is adamant about wanting to attend. He tells his parents all of his friends are going to the concert and one night won't make a difference even with the work he has to do.

After listening carefully to what Barry has to say, his father responds, "We understand that this concert is very important to you—as are your friends. You know your mother and I want you to have as many positive experiences this year as possible, including concerts. We realize that the concert is an hour away, all of your friends will be there and that this is the only appearance of the band probably until the spring. We also know how important school is to you—as is getting into the college that you have chosen—all of which depends upon the grades you get and your SAT scores. If this concert were on a Friday or Saturday, there would be no question about giving you permission to attend.

Through no fault of your own, your health issues put you behind where you would normally be academically. Your mom and I appreciate your hard work in trying to catch up. We recognize you want to go to the concert with your friends and that you understand you need to stay on deadline with the paper assignments. Did I leave anything out or did I sum things up pretty well?"

Whatever decision is made from this point forward, Barry would certainly have to concede that his parents are being thoughtful and sensitive to the situation. This type of repeating back what parents hear can be quite effective in preventing an argument because their child knows he has indeed been heard. If parents make this effort, they will succeed in overcoming a good deal of resistance from their children.

An additional benefit for negotiating with your child is the creation of an atmosphere of openness, which will allow your child to feel comfortable talking about issues with you in the future. Clearly, the Internet presents as many dangers as opportunities for socialization and educational growth. A number of significant points have to be made with your child—mainly in the area of safety. It is critical that your child understand he can approach and talk with you when he feels uneasy about something he sees on the Internet. Build on this safety valve because, when it comes down to it, what parents really want is to protect their children from harm.

Peers and media bias toward the advantages and fun associated with Internet and cell phone use will fuel your child's cognitive bias. Your child uses technology to connect and share information, day and night, with other children. Your child's circle of friends is seldom out of sight. Cell phones can be taken to bed and friends texted without parents hearing a sound. Children do not see the danger in being accessible twenty-four hours a day, nor do they see the danger in giving away information about themselves or sending photos to others.

On the other hand, parents' cognitive bias is more directed by media warnings and concerns about the use of cell phone and Internet use. They hear warnings about children waking up exhausted, children's grades slipping because of failure to turn in assignments on time, children at risk for kidnapping and pedophiles, and children acting secretively when using a computer. As a result of these warnings, fact and fiction need to be distinguished. The issue of cognitive bias—for and against

Internet and cell phone use—should be discussed in the context of the concerns that both parents and children have with regard to these matters. Parents can frankly admit that they have a bias based upon the safety of their children.

Internet and cell phone use has all the earmarks of being a hot topic in any household. The child's confirmation bias will most likely center on the beneficial effects as they quote teachers and other sources that support technology's constructive effects. Everything the child sees in school, in movies, and on TV confirms the inevitability and usefulness of texting and social media. Contrary to the child's assessment, parents refer to articles that show that children are spending inordinate amounts of time using these technologies and, as a result, are becoming less rather than more social. If battle lines are drawn and the parent and child come to an impasse, the situation must be reframed and a viable contract must be negotiated.

How Does a Negotiation Begin?

How can two people who seem to be so opposed to the other's point of view come to an agreement? To begin, the parent might tell a story that illustrates negotiation. Let's take a look at a movie titled *The Paper Chase*. It is based on a 1970s novel and tells the story of a first-year Harvard law student, James Hart, and his struggles to succeed in a difficult course in contracts. The film features the riveting character of Professor Charles Kingsfield (played by John Houseman in an Academy Award–winning performance). Professor Kingsfield, in the movie version, is portrayed as a cold, aloof, and severe teacher. In the later spinoff of *The Paper Chase* as a television series, that started on CBS and then went to SHO, the character of Professor Kingsfield (again played by John Houseman) is humanized a great deal as a teacher and as a person. In the series, episodes utilized the vehicle of contract writing to demonstrate how contracts will work as an important tool in everyone's life.

As it is apparently done in law school classes, Professor Kingsfield would ask questions directed at specific students, to which the student would frequently give the wrong answer. In one episode, Professor Kingsfield asked the student "What is meant by a meeting of the minds?" The student incorrectly responds, "Two minds in agreement." to which the professor corrects the student by saying, "No, two minds in disagreement." The professor explains that the *best* contracts are made between people who have the biggest disagreements—because of the need to be specific in spelling out what one person wants from the other.

Cognitive Bias and Changing Someone's Mind Can Be Frustrating
What we know about cognitive bias would indicate that trying to change someone else's mind is an endeavor in frustration. So, rather than argue to change the other person's mind, begin by *agreeing to disagree.* Work from there to see if a suitable agreement can be reached. Using a story like *The Paper Chase* to begin the negotiation can save a great deal of frustration because it is able to show that people with very different points of view can still negotiate and come to mutually beneficial agreements.

Parents Want and Need to Express Concerns
Parents wonder if their children are entering chat rooms, who they are speaking with and what they are talking about. Parents want their children to be aware of Internet predators who pose as teenagers. Parents want to warn their children to never meet with someone they have met online. And, they also want them to be aware that once something is posted on the Internet, it is in the public domain—and can never be erased. Parents want their children to think things through before responding to text messages, and be released from the constant pressure of having to immediately respond.

Another area of growing parental concern is cyberbullying. Unlike the predator that may be unknown to the child, the cyberbully often is someone the child knows from school.

Cyberbullying trains and exposes children to reveal personal information, send or forward demeaning text messages, and post photos of the child without their consent. Cyberbullying encourages the spreading of lies and rumors, and affects children online and offline as well. Unlike the usual schoolyard bullying, cyberbullying is a great deal more difficult to avoid. Cyberbullying does not end when the child comes home from school. It continues throughout day and night—anytime or anyplace. Avoiding cyberbullying is not as easy as parents would like to think. When a child hears, "Don't open your messages," a child's curiosity often compels him to open messages to see what other people are saying about him.

A Child Is Often Resistant to Negotiation

Because children are so caught up in social media, they are very likely to want to ignore advice. They tend to see only the upside of communicating with peers—not what the longer-term effects about what they say and what others say about them might bring. A common defense a child might bring to the negotiation table falls under the category of *victimization*. Children have a way of presenting problems to parents in the form of victimization: "You're not being fair," or "You don't trust me!" In both statements, the child implies that she is a victim of an unfair and mistrusting parent. What parent wants to be seen as unfair, a tyrant, or suspicious and mistrusting? Of course no self-respecting parent would want to be characterized this way. As a parent, how do you respond to these charges leveled against you? Reframing—this is where it comes into play.

Since no one can disprove a negative—a parent cannot prove that he is fair or unfair, or trusting or mistrusting. However, the accusation can be reframed by saying, "You're right, I'm not fair. I'm too generous when it comes to you. I have frequently given things away simply because you have asked for them. Now, that's not fair because that misleads you into thinking that very little in this world has to be earned. My fault is in being overly generous."

162

With regard to your child's statement "You don't trust me!" try to make your child understand that trust is not something that is extended in a gratuitous fashion but rather trust is earned. A response could go something like this, "Trust is something that one earns when one's behavior is consistent with the promises that have been made. If your behavior is always consistent with your word, I cannot do anything else but trust you. Whether you see me as trusting you or not—trust resides in *you*, not in me. If you give me your word and you live up to your word, you will have earned my trust." Each new request for trust is dependent upon past behavior. It is an ongoing process.

Consistent with confirmation bias, the parent cannot order the child to change his mind. Instead, the parent should redirect the child's attention to the child's words and behavior while addressing the issues at hand. Avoid victim-like assertions by your child and present alternatives that empower your child to be a responsible individual by offering choices to make. As a parent, do not take a defensive position by answering questions that cannot be proven or disproven. Questions should always be meant to obtain answers— not to confound the other individual by playing a form of gotcha. Adhere to the rule: *Whoever is asking the questions is in charge; whoever has to answer questions is clearly not in charge.* When a parent tries to answer victim questions, the child is placed in charge and the parent will paradoxically become the victim.

Supervise the Use of Your Child's Time
It should be made clear from the outset that parental supervision is not part of the negotiation. Parents have the right and the duty to supervise or control their child's use of time. The issue is the practical application of supervision and how much freedom the child should be allowed.

Ask Questions
A parent should ask his child for a list of regularly scheduled activities and an accounting of the amount of time spent on each

activity. "How much time is devoted to homework? How much time is associated with communicating with friends? What seems to be a reasonable time limit to stop communicating toward the end of the day?" The answers provided by your child can then be reviewed and new questions brought up. If the time for socializing is out of proportion with the time devoted to homework, more questions can be raised with your child as to how this allocation of time is beneficial or not. Consistent with negotiation, the parent wants to hear what his child is saying—and should be ready to repeat back what is heard in a patient and understanding manner. The parent may not agree with the child's initial request but at no juncture should a parent enter into a lecture. Ask questions to further define present and future situations.

If you find yourself at an impasse, the negotiation can be stopped and you can think out loud. "Let me see if I understand your position." State your child's position in a fair and concise fashion and give him time to think over what he is asking before he comes back with an alternative proposal. Also, as an example, if inappropriate Internet use is the issue, you can ask your child to research resources that provide additional information regarding Internet safety. "If you can provide me with safety features that you intend to use, I would be inclined to think you can use the technologies you have at your disposal in an intelligent way."

Tell Stories to Highlight Issues: Watch a Film Together

Rather than quoting numerous statistics to a child, it is likely to be more effective to utilize film as a way of getting an idea across. Just as the book and film *The Diary of Anne Frank* tells the story of the persecution of thousands of people through the eyes of one young girl, cyberbullying and its effect on a person can be captured in a realistic way by watching a made-for-TV movie titled *Cyberbully*.

Cyberbully is the story of a teenage girl named Taylor who, as a result of an offhand comment to a classmate, becomes the focus of cyberbullying. Taylor becomes increasingly isolated as the object of vicious rumors that were started by some of her former friends. The abuse that Taylor received is so oppressive that she impulsively attempts suicide. When Taylor fails to get the lid off the container of pills she tries to use, her dilemma is discovered and she is hospitalized. Taylor's mother approaches the school system, and gets Taylor involved in a support group.

A movie is a great tool for parents to use when discussing a myriad of issues including this topic. Without doubt, Taylor's frustration is palpable as she is attacked anonymously by a wide variety of people who are protected by legal loopholes that allow cyberbullying. While *Cyberbully* has a happy ending, the emotional torture that Taylor experiences is profound. Now, while most children would think that this would never happen to them—the possibilities for cyberbullying are very real. The film certainly affected many people. It was the second-most viewed TV movie of the 2010 and 2011 season.

After watching a movie, a parent can think out loud about the meaning of it. Equally important is for the parent to ask questions as a way to have his child internalize its message. Because the type of trap that Taylor fell into is so subtle and insidious, parents need to set up regular family meetings to discuss online topics. It's also imperative to check privacy settings and online profiles for inappropriate posts on websites. Through ongoing mutual communication between you and your child, always emphasis how activities should foster growth and maturity.

Chapter 14 Questions

Am I creating the opportunity for negotiation?

Am I handling the "You don't trust me!" statement effectively?

Am I using stories and movies effectively?

Am I being open in my approach to discussion?

Chapter 15

CONFRONTATION: ITS POSITIVE USE

Whenever the term *confrontation* comes up in conversation, there is almost always an immediate reaction on the part of someone to say, "I don't like confrontations." Often, confrontations bring to mind expressions of anger in which one person has "had enough" and begins to scream and rant at another—or is on the brink of doing so. It is true that many confrontations are usually somewhat aggressive in nature. Scenes of confrontations in films usually portray dramatic moments. After all, what's the box-office appeal of a movie in which people settle disagreements intelligently and peacefully? The common view of confrontations is one of face-to-face, tension-filled meetings between people with strong unconstructive feelings toward one another.

While confrontations are most often thought of as a negative, confrontations can also be invitations for growth and the development of relationships. There is a type of confrontation in which one person says to another, "I love you,"—a statement that is bound to draw a response from the other person. The "I love you" comment may be a hold-your-breath moment since you are not sure what kind of reaction you may get!

Confrontations are usually associated with highly charged emotional situations in which a person does one of the following:
1. Freezes to consider options and then either discharges energy by:
    a. running away (flight); or
    b. fight as a last resort.

Fortunately, for thinking creatures such as us, there is another option.

2. Freeze and after freezing—there is an encounter of insight.

Insight is the ability to understand the connections between words and behaviors. Insight enables us to think through problems and determine how possible solutions can be applied. Insight is the ability to learn from mistakes. Parents have the responsibility to help foster insight in their children. Often this is accomplished though confrontation and it is important for the parent to make confrontations safe encounters. It begins with decreasing the anxiety associated with a confrontation by the parent remaining in control.

Can confrontation be handled without threatening or feeling threatened? There may be no way to eliminate completely a sense of threat but there are definitely ways to minimize it, as can be seen in the following exchange.

Stuart's parents received a report from their child's school indicating he had not turned in several homework assignments. This was not a first-time occurrence. On two previous occasions, Stuart's parents discussed the matter with Stuart and he contended that it was just a mix-up and that he had turned in the assignments: Nevertheless, he promised it would not happen again. The parents contacted the school and spoke with the teacher. Not only was Stuart not doing the assigned homework; he was also falling behind in class.

Stuart's parents were also concerned about the amount of time that he was spending on the computer playing games and texting back and forth with his classmates. Stuart's parents decided to have a serious meeting with him about his overall approach to schoolwork. They wondered about the change in Stuart's behavior. Previously he had been a diligent student. Stuart's parents were determined to get him to talk about what was going on since only Stuart knew the answers to their questions. They wanted to head off the problem before it became bigger—and they were determined to do it in a helpful and nonthreatening way. Previous lectures and threats of restricting his computer and cell phone time had failed. Stuart had simply nodded his head in agreement, promised he would do better and promptly seemed to forget his promise.

Stuart's parents were very frustrated but had learned that raising their voice and lecturing did not work. Understanding that lectures followed by threats only produce defensive reactions, they were determined this time around not to let their frustration turn into an attack on Stuart. A child in this type of situation usually defends himself by saying how unfair his parents are and that the teacher gives too much work. The more a child defends himself with this style, the more he reinforces the idea that he is being picked on unfairly.

To avoid defensive communication, don't revert to talking about past history. It will not undo whatever went wrong. Obviously the past has to be acknowledged in that Stuart had not been turning in assignments, as he should. However, once he acknowledges the problem, no further criticism should be given—no accusatory statements like, "How could you be so stupid?" or "Are you too lazy to do a few simple assignments?" To vent in this way might feel good at the moment to the frustrated parent, but it will produce a negative pushback, as the child likely will view himself as the victim.

Once problems are acknowledged, address solutions for the present and discuss the changes that must be made going forward into future situations. When a child takes responsibility for his behavior, the parents' focus should be on the changes that need to be made to prevent similar situations from occurring in the future. Parents do not want a paradigm created that establishes a principle based on fighting back. If a person feels attacked, the principle "You attack and I'll defend!" is set into motion. This is definitely not a good direction in which to head.

In Stuart's situation, suppose the parents were to say, "I think we agree you have been having a problem getting your assignments turned in on time. I don't want to get into why that happened. Rather, I want to hear what your plan is for the future so that you will be able to get your assignments turned in on time as your teacher directs. What changes will you have to make to get this done?"

Remember, don't get mired about what has been done in the past; but rather focus on what needs to get done now. You also want to hear what your child is going to do going forward. You want your child to share in problem solving—not problem defending. It is important that your child verbalize the right things to do. Why is that? The child is taking ownership of the problem and the resolution when he hears himself saying the words.

Stay Out of the Past

While working at a therapeutic school, I was walking by a classroom just after an altercation had occurred between two elementary school children. Apparently, one of the children, angered at the other, had picked up a short block of wood and threw it at the other child. As I was passing the classroom door, I heard the teacher ask the child, "Why did you throw a block of wood at that child?"

In an attempt to justify his behavior, the child immediately began to describe what the other child had done to him that called for retaliation. The teacher continued asking questions in an apparent attempt to understand why the behavior had occurred. The child continued to defend his behavior.

After the teacher had finished her conversation with the child, I returned to the classroom to suggest a different approach in the future when dealing with this type of circumstance. I pointed out that by asking the question, "Why did you do that?" the teacher was inviting the child to give a defense of his own behavior perhaps resulting in "locking in" a negative behavior that the teacher did not want repeated.

The teacher unknowingly reinforced the wrong behavior by allowing the child to verbalize the wrong behavior. Instead of asking, "Why did you do that?" I suggested that in a future similar situation, the teacher should ask a different type of question; such as, "Do you know you could have injured the other child and do you understand there is no excuse for that kind of aggressive behavior?" The teacher should wait for an answer. Once the child admits that his behavior was dangerous, the teacher is in a good position to ask, "Tell me how you can handle your anger in the future toward another student in a safer way?"

Arrest the Behavior

The first step in arresting negative behavior is to ask a question—not about an act of provocation on the part of the other child, but rather about the aggressive and dangerous behavior that followed in response. This type of question changes the focus of the exchange.

As a parent, you do not want to hear what went wrong and why your child felt justified in assaulting another child. You want an acknowledgment from your child about his incorrect response and you want to hear how your child will handle negative situations in the future. Your next question is, "What should you do when someone is provoking you? Do you think you should handle it yourself or report it to one of your parents or your teacher?"

Deliberately ask questions that will pull for positive responses. Lock in the correct behavior by asking questions and listening to answers. Apply the phenomenon of cognitive dissonance—it is very difficult to say something convincingly if you do not believe what you are saying. For cognitive dissonance to work, you want your child to hear himself acknowledge the benefit of positive responses to negative situations.

Redirect Negative Behavior by Criticizing in a Positive Way

The problem with many criticisms is that they are delivered within the context of the problem that has just occurred without regard to the larger context of the more global relationship between the parties. A person who feels slighted or hurt may immediately react with a hurtful response. A person receiving the criticism often focuses on the injustice of the remark and, when this is the case, an explosive exchange often follows.

"How could you have been so thoughtless not to have called when you knew you would be late? Sometimes you are so irresponsible," says the injured person. Don't ignore that the act may well be a single instance in an otherwise positive relationship. If you do, the person receiving the criticism may well respond by saying, "Why are you always overreacting and trying to control me? Other parents don't overreact over the littlest things like you do."

If you fall into this trap, the battle lines are drawn and reason is put on hold while the parties begin assembling a laundry list of past transgressions. How long will the negative dialogue continue and how many other insults will be exchanged before reason becomes part of the discussion?

It is important to understand that many problems can be avoided by praise and positively phrased criticisms and recommendations from the parent. This is where the parent can make great use out of such nondirective techniques as: Thinking Out Loud and Telling Stories. The process of getting the behavior you want often can be accomplished by using a criticism in a four-part statement delivered as though it was a single statement. The four-part statement I am proposing is a very positive way to get what you want without having the other person react negatively and rebel against what you're saying. An effective criticism does not have to be hurtful or negative.

The Four-Part Positive Criticism Preserves the Wider Context of a Relationship

The importance of the four-part statement known as a Positive Criticism cannot be overemphasized. Mastering this technique may well negate the need to practice some of the more difficult techniques to be described. The four-step criticism should be delivered sequentially as outlined below.

Positive Criticism Includes the Following Four Elements:

1. feeling (global feeling about how you appreciate the other person)

2. behavior (the negative behavior is cited)
3. behavior (the positive behavior that you would like to see is defined)
4. feeling (a feeling that shows appreciation for their attention)

The first step—expressing a global feeling—is crucial for a number of reasons that affect both the child and the parent. The child is affected because he hears the parent acknowledge him as someone who is of value and who is loved and appreciated. The parent is affected because by putting his feelings for the child into words, he reminds himself what the child means to him. As a result, whatever the parent views as the transgression is now relative to the parent's overall appreciation of his child as a person. By reminding himself of his child's value, the parent is less likely to make an offensive statement.

For example, suppose you do not like the quality of work your child has done on a school assignment. The process should take place as follows: "John, I generally like (feeling) the work that you do and appreciate the effort you put into it. This assignment is not up to your usual quality (behavior). The previous assignments you have been doing (behavior) are much neater and the quality of work very good. I know you can do better if you're willing to put time into this project. Why don't you give it another try and bring the quality of the work up to your usual standard. I appreciate (feeling) your efforts and I'm looking forward to reading the revised version."

Usually, the child receiving the criticism reacts quite positively because he hears *the first part (feeling) and the last two parts (the behavior you expect and your feeling) more clearly than the second part that sounds more critical.* The child especially hears the part about the usual high quality of work and how the parent feels about him. The child is encouraged. If your child begins to talk about how difficult it is to redo the assignment, you should again reinforce what a great job your child has done in the past.

This type of criticism is simple and it will work if you practice the delivery until it flows easily. It may not come quickly because it takes practice. With practice you will become professional. Someone once said that a professional is someone who has done something difficult over and over again until it appears easy. Like the professional, you must practice your technique many times before you get good at it.

Chapter 15 Questions

Am I working at decreasing anxiety, when I use confrontation?

Am I staying out of the past and focusing on the future when I correct?

Am I arresting the negative behavior?

Am I using a four-part form of correction (feeling, behavior, behavior, feeling)?

Chapter 16

RELAPSE AND SUMMARY OF SKILLS

In an earlier chapter, we looked at the story of Chris, who had lied to his parents about attending a party at the home of a friend where there was no parental supervision. Chris's parents confronted him and, after an internal struggle, he admitted what he had done. Chris promised he would no longer attend parentally unsupervised parties. Chris made good on his promise for several weeks. He spent time at the homes of friends and, on occasion, stayed overnight. Chris would check in with his parents to let them know that his friends' parents were present during his visits. They felt reassured that responsible parents were supervising their son and noticed that Chris was being diligent in doing his schoolwork. Things appeared to be going well. Several weeks later, Chris's parents got a call from another boy's mother who told them of an unsupervised party that both her son and Chris had attended. The mother had learned that drugs and alcohol were present and may have been used by some of the children. Chris's parents were faced with the fact that Chris had lied and relapsed into negative behavior.

Should a Relapse Be Expected?
A relapse is a fairly common occurrence and can happen without warning. Just when a parent begins to think that things have turned around and everything is running smoothly suddenly, their child reverts back to the previous behavior. After all the

hard work communicating and negotiating, things seem to fall apart. When a relapse happens, a parent is likely to be quite upset and is inclined to act out with an angry outburst. The parent most likely wants to scream, "We had an agreement, didn't we? How could you do this again after giving your word?" The parent is faced with a choice to make—be quite reactive to the situation and, after an angry outburst, spend a great deal of time wondering why it happened—or skip the outburst and move on to figure out what to do.

What Do You Do When a Relapse Occurs?

The better scenario, when faced with figuring out how to handle the relapse, is based on the expectation that a relapse is likely to occur. A relapse is to be expected—it is almost inevitable that it will happen. The expectation that it will likely occur does not negate that it will be upsetting but, if handled well, it will just be a bump in the road—and could lead to much better outcomes in the future. Relapse in a family situation has often been described in a parallel way to symptoms after physical medical recoveries. How many times has someone come down with the flu, thought he had completely recovered, gone out to do too much too soon only to find himself back in bed again with a reoccurrence of flu symptoms? While the second-time-around recovery period is usually short-lived the patient may be on the edge of despair and believes he will never fully recover.

All Is Not Lost When a Child Relapses

If and when there is a relapse, it is the parent who *anticipates* a relapse who is likely to remain calmer than the parent who does not believe that a relapse is possible. To jump-start the treatment of the problem begin with the statement, "We've had a relapse—we need to address it, deal with it, and correct it." The relapse is a relative event and should never be regarded as though it's an absolute situation—an "always-was and always-will-be condition." It happened. Avoid the "all is lost" mentality. A relapse has a beginning and it will have an end. Approach the relapse in the context, "We have had a slip. We need to go back to work and agree to straighten this all out so that we can move forward." However, at the very beginning, it should be made clear that your child's behavior is not negotiable—it must be improved.

Stay In Control

To handle a relapse effectively, the parent must maintain control—not of how he feels—but of how he handles and expresses his feelings. The parent can and should talk about his upset but not act out his upset. View the relapse and how you handle it as another chance to have a teaching moment—put feelings into words; do not act out on feelings. Stay in control and remember it is against the rebellious behaviors that you are directing your attention—not the child. If you do direct your displeasure to the child, you create a child who is demeaned and you label him a failure. You have only succeeded in pouring more fuel on the fire. If you act out, expect your child to act out in return. Ask yourself: What have you gained? If you have a temper tantrum, you have given your child license to have a temper tantrum. Remember, it is up to the parent to model good behavior. Your child will imitate negative as well as positive behavior.

Work It Out Together

Let's circle back to Chris. How did this relapse happen? Was it a question of Chris's judgment taking a backseat to his impulses? Did Chris overrate his ability to engage in a situation and not get caught—or did he simply not think through the consequences of his actions? Did Chris go along with his friends for fear of their reaction if he did not follow their lead? Everyone needs self-confidence or self-efficacy. Social psychologists have referred to this terminology as the individual's belief in his ability to deal effectively with a variety of situations. A positive sense of self-efficacy plays a vital role in the development of one's feelings about self and affects later success in achieving life goals. When self-efficacy is low, a child tends to avoid challenges and focuses on personal failings and negative outcomes. A child with low self-efficacy can lose confidence in his personal abilities to succeed. Confrontation should not be crushing. As a parent, you do not want your child to feel incompetent and a failure and yet you must set limits and teach the value of living up to one's word. As a parent, you must *teach your child to learn and recover from mistakes.*

The Notion of Failure Is Up to the Individual

The line "Failure is not an option" comes from the 1995 movie *Apollo 13*. The story is about a space mission to land on the moon. From the beginning of the mission, things go wrong. When there is an oxygen tank explosion on board the spacecraft, the mission is immediately aborted. For the astronauts, that is not the worst of it. They have to get home alive on the crippled spacecraft. In the film, the flight director at Mission Control (played by Ed Harris) gathers his staff of engineers together and delivers the message, "We have never lost an American in space and we're sure as hell not going to lose one on my watch! Failure is not an option!"

What makes the film so riveting, besides getting Tom Hanks back from outer space alive, is the ingenious work of the engineers to overcome all obstacles to produce a makeshift solution that actually worked. When the real-life flight director, Gene Kranz, was asked if there were times when everybody, or some, panicked his answer was, "No, when bad things happened, we calmly laid out all the options, and failure was not one of them. We never panicked, and we never gave up on finding a solution."

Failure happens only when one does not try to overcome obstacles. There is always a way to succeed. All set backs are recoverable. Failure only occurs when a person believes he is defeated and stops trying. Everyone experiences defeats in life but the only defeat that cannot be overcome is the one in which the individual puts forth no effort to succeed.

Tap into Control and Composure

In order to create a win-win situation, draw confidence from the considerable set of tools at your disposal. As a parent, *tune into* the power you possess. Have a talk with yourself before confrontations. Remind yourself that you have all the rewards to give and that your child wants and needs these rewards. *Believe* that no matter what your child might say, the issue will not change until the problem is resolved. When a relapse occurs remind your child how well things were going and that his behavior must get back to where it was before the slip. Reinforce that your child was able to show improvement and this must reoccur. Keep in the forefront of your mind that the problem is the child's behavior—not the child. Your *confidence* in yourself—and in your ability to find a solution—will erode resistance.

Keep telling yourself that persistence overcomes resistance and never pay emotionally for your child's misbehavior. Always remember the analogy of learning how to ski—when you feel like you are speeding down a slippery slope out of control—sit back on your skis. Apply the brakes. Take a moment to reflect before responding. Do not simply react. Concentrate on the misbehavior. Treat it objectively. Look at the behavior as if it is an object to be studied, e.g., what specifically is my child doing wrong?

Get the Excuses Out of the Way

Suppose your child starts asking you questions about why he has to follow what he thinks are overly strict rules that are not imposed on his friends—and asks you to explain the rationale for your decisions. Do you go there? Do you think your child really wants to hear your position to understand you better? Or, does he want to hear your explanation so that he can better position himself for an argument with you? Whatever you say, be prepared to hear that your ideas are old-fashioned. Don't take the bait. Once you begin to answer a series of *why* questions, you will probably lose—and you are likely to hear yourself echo the words of parental absolute finality: "Because I said so, that's why!"

What Is an Alternative Way to Answer a "Why" Question?

Begin by saying: "I find that when someone asks me 'why?' it is usually for one of two reasons:

1. They want to understand the basis for my decision; or
2. They want to argue with me to get me to change my mind.

Now, if you want to understand my concerns and the basis for my thinking, I would be glad to answer your question. However, if you're asking me why so you can argue with me—that will not work and I will stop talking. In addition, the next time you ask me why, I will suspect, based on past experience, that you are not doing it to understand my reasoning but rather to argue. If I feel that is the case, again I probably will not give you an explanation. So, do you still want to know why?" At this point your child will most likely mutter "Never mind."

If your child indicates he wants to continue the conversation, go ahead and answer the *why* question. It gives you a chance to *think out loud* and maybe even tell a relevant story. After all, if you're going to ask your child why he is doing something, is it not only fair to give the child insight into your thinking? In saying this, remember the principle—whoever is asking the question is in control—and conversely, whoever has to answer the questions is clearly *not* in charge. The point: Do not let your child control the discussion. If so, you will place yourself on the defensive by answering questions. It is your child who owes the explanation.

Focus on Behavior

In Chris's case, there were two issues that needed to be addressed: 1. Chris went to a house where there was no parental supervision; and 2. after he promised his parents that he would not go to parentally unsupervised homes in the future, he failed to live up to his word. Whatever a parent's first reaction is to a child's negative behavior, parents need to avoid getting into the nonproductive lecture mode. A parent's first reaction most likely will be feelings of betrayal. However, of critical concern is the process of your child's growth and development. Since development is a marathon, not a sprint, learning to negotiate with your child for the long run is important.

In taking corrective action, keep the focus on your child's performance and on the specific behavior that failed to meet the agreed-upon standard. Make it clear that expected improvement is a must—it is nonnegotiable. At the outset, the focus must be kept strictly on the lack of improvement since the previous meeting. You do not want to hear your child's excuses; but rather, you want to hear the cause of the violation of trust.

As soon as the causes of problems are stated, the focus of the meeting should shift to the future. You must ask for your child's help in offering ideas to solve problems. Discuss together: What action will the child take to prevent problems in the future? What will the child do to assure his parents that something constructive has been learned from the situation? Together, identify high-risk situations. Ask your child if he is able to identify and cope with these situations.

Owning the Solution to a Problem Lends Value

There is an old saying, "Good judgment is based on experience and experience is based on bad judgment." When children make bad judgments, parents must help children take ownership of solutions. A child must learn to place problem resolution into her personal experience, which will, in turn, help her develop the strong moral compass required to make good judgments in the future.

The more a child owns the solution to a problem, the more she is likely to value the solution. It is one thing for a parent to state a solution. It is quite another matter—and one of far greater value—if the child were to say the same thing as the parent. A parent should wait for her child to offer solutions. If the parent suggests solutions, it should be done in an open-ended assertive way that cannot be responded to by the child with a simple yes or no. It should be done in a way that will draw the child out in an attempt to discover what has gone wrong.

Parents, along with their children, should examine the triggers that lead to relapse. What are the barriers to success? Lead your child to the pathways of self-examination: "What things do you need to do to be seen as a person of your word and as someone people will respect? What choices need to be made going forward?"

Be empathetic about the problem, yet persistent about the behavior and the change that is required. Your child is responsible for thinking through her behavior and making the necessary changes. In keeping with the rules of negotiation, listen carefully and be ready to repeat back to her what you have heard. In repeating back her words and interpreting her thoughts, be sure to do so in a very positive way indicating that you understand. In addition, present your child's point of view in an even more positive light than your child used. As we have read by examples in previous chapters, successful negotiation greatly reduces arguing because your child understands that you are making an effort to really understand what she is saying.

Change Your Perception of the Child's Behavior in a Positive Way

Remember "The Dead Man Rule": Do not state a desired behavior in a negative way. Virtually every negative statement fails the Dead Man Rule. Never ask anyone to do something if a dead man could do it better. A directive that says, "Don't run," fails the Dead Man Rule because 100 percent of the time a dead man will not run. Instead, if you want someone to walk, simply say, "Please walk."

A parent should want to hear goals that are stated positively and can be measured. Emphasis should be placed on the idea that a relapse can be remedied. Give credit for compliance that the child demonstrated prior to the relapse. Establish new goals in light of what the child has learned about himself. Shift the focus away from failure in an encouraging environment to promote problem solving. Support and energize the child with regard to the process of making positive change.

When your child is able to verbalize and internalize effective coping strategies to deal with high-risk situations, the probability of relapse will likely decrease significantly. Also, coping effectively with high-risk situations is likely to increase the child's sense of worth and autonomy. By enabling your child to verbalize beliefs regarding his ability to affect positive change, his self-confidence to face challenges competently and make intelligent mature choices in life is strongly affected.

Resistance and Milton Erickson

The famous therapist Milton Erickson saw great value in relapse. Dr. Erickson viewed relapse as a way to bypass simple unthinking short-lived "obedience and compliance." He felt that compliant people were more prone to relapse in the absence of the therapeutic process. As a result, Dr. Erickson occasionally arranged for patients to fail in an attempt to improve and reinforce the benefit of successful negotiating techniques.

Dr. Erickson believed that failure was part of life, and in an individual's fragile state of learning to live, think, and behave differently, a random therapeutic unsupervised failure might prove catastrophic. Deliberately causing a relapse allowed Erickson to control the variables of that failure, and to cast the relapse in a positive perspective for the patient.

The point is not to encourage relapse; but rather, to view relapse as a part of growth and development. Falling down is not a problem; not knowing how to get back up is a problem. The key to success is not to let setbacks undermine your child's self-confidence. If the child lapses back to a former negative behavior, take a hard look at why it happened and develop a plan to move forward. While there is no doubt that relapses can be difficult, the best solution is to start again, properly prepared with action steps within your resources and commitment to your goals. Your child needs to learn how to deal with future temptations that he can build on to create future successes. Give your child what he needs—share your toolbox.

A relapse is not the end.
    Begin again.
        The sooner you begin, the sooner the relapse will end.
            Life will go on—
                And, it will be better.

Chapter 16 Questions

Do I see a relapse as an opportunity to further my child's development?

Do I see relapse as a relative event?

Am I asking the right questions following a relapse?

Am I encouraging my child to keep trying?

ABOUT THE AUTHOR

James F. McTamney graduated from Catholic University of America in 1976 with a PhD in psychology. For thirty years, he has worked extensively with children and families in hospitals and clinics and in a private-practice setting. Dr. McTamney has taught college courses and conducted workshops for parents and other professionals and has been a lecturer and former president for the Baltimore Psychological Association. Dr. McTamney has experience supervising psychology interns and psychiatric residents in behavioral approaches to helping difficult children in a variety of settings and situations. In his lectures and workshops, he merges cognitive behavioral principles with communication skills to give people understanding into the dynamics of interpersonal interactions along with the tools needed to succeed in teaching and maintaining values in their children.

RESOURCES

Films
- *A River Runs Through It* (1992). A film based on a true story about two boys, Norman and Paul, growing up in Montana. One is rebellious of his father, Reverend Maclean, a Presbyterian minister, while the other is studious and has his feet on the ground. The film follows their coming of age in the Rocky Mountain region during a span of time from roughly World War I to the early days of the Great Depression. The one love both boys have is fly-fishing.
- *Apollo 13* (1995). A film based on the true story of the ill-fated 13th Apollo mission bound for the moon. Astronauts Lovell, Haise, and Swigert were scheduled to fly *Apollo 14*, but are moved up to *13*. It's 1970, and America has already achieved its lunar landing goal, so there's little interest in this "routine" flight until things go very wrong and prospects of a safe return are jeopardized.
- *Better Off Dead* (1985). Lane Meyer is a depressed teen who loses his girlfriend, Beth. Lane is left alone and thinks up treacherous ways of killing himself. Simultaneously, he must endure his mother's terrible cooking, which literally slides off the table, and his disgusting next-door neighbor Ricky (and Ricky's mom) while he prepares for the skiing race of his life—to get his old girlfriend back!

- *Butch Cassidy and the Sundance Kid* (1969). Butch and Sundance are the two leaders of the Hole-in-the-Wall Gang. Butch is all ideas; Sundance is all action and skill. The West is becoming civilized and when Butch and Sundance rob a train once too often, a special posse begins trailing them no matter where they run. The film is based on the exploits of the historical characters.

- *Carnage* (2011). Two sets of parents hold a cordial meeting after their sons are involved in a fight, though as their time together progresses, increasingly childish behavior throws the discussion into chaos.

- *Catch-22* (1970). A man is trying desperately to be certified insane during World War II so he can stop flying missions.

- *Diary of Anne Frank* (1959). A harrowing story of a young Jewish girl who, with her family and their friends, is forced into hiding in an attic in Nazi-occupied Amsterdam.

- *Full Metal Jacket* (1987). A pragmatic US Marine observes the dehumanizing effects the United States-Vietnam War has on his fellow recruits from their brutal boot camp training to the bloody street fighting in Hue.

- *Ordinary People* (1980). The accidental death of the older son of an affluent family deeply strains the relationships among the bitter mother, the good-natured father, and the guilt-ridden younger son.

- *Red Badge of Courage* (1951). A truncated adaptation of Stephen Crane's novel about a Union soldier who struggles to find the courage to fight in the heat of battle during the Civil War.

- *The Shawshank Redemption* (1994). Two imprisoned men bond over a number of years, finding solace and eventual redemption through acts of common decency.

- *Silence of the Lambs* (1991). A young FBI cadet must confide in an incarcerated and manipulative killer to receive his help on catching another serial killer who skins his victims.

- *Thank You for Smoking* (2005). This satirical comedy follows the machinations of Big Tobacco's chief spokesman, Nick Naylor, who spins on behalf of cigarettes while trying to remain a role model for his twelve-year-old son.

- *The Godfather* (1972). The aging patriarch of an organized crime dynasty transfers control of his clandestine empire to his reluctant son. The clash of the Don's fading old world values and the new ways will demand a terrible price, especially from protagonist Michael Corleone, all for the sake of the family.

- *The Paper Chase* (1973). A serious, hard-working student, James T. Hart faces the rigors of his first year at Harvard Law School. The pressure to succeed is tremendous and some of the students form study groups while also spending a great many hours studying. Hart's greatest challenge is contract law and his professor Charles W. Kingsfield, Jr. Using the Socratic Method, Kingsfield challenges his students with questions demanding accuracy and creativity in their responses and often humiliating those who are unable to respond.

- *To Kill a Mockingbird* (1962). A film based on Harper Lee's Pulitzer Prize–winning book of 1961. Atticus Finch is a lawyer in a racially divided Alabama town in the 1930s. He agrees to defend a young black man who is accused of raping a white woman. Many of the townspeople try to get Atticus to pull out of the trial, but he decides to go ahead. How will the trial turn out—and will it change any of the racial tension in the town?

Books:

- Festinger, Leon. *A Theory of Cognitive Dissonance.* (Stanford University Press, 1962.) Dr. Festinger's theory of cognitive dissonance has been widely recognized for its important and influential concepts in areas of motivation and social psychology. The theory of dissonance is here applied to the problem of why partial reward, delay of reward, and effort expenditure during training result in increased resistance to extinction. The author contends that a state of impasse exists within learning theory largely because some of its major assumptions stand in apparent opposition to certain well-established experimental results. The book puts forward a new theory that seems to reconcile these data and assumptions.

- Fisher, Roger and Ury, William. *Getting to Yes: Negotiating Agreement Without Giving In.* (First published by Houghton Mifflin, 1983. Published by Penguin Books, 1991.) Based on the work of the Harvard Negotiation Project, a group that deals with all levels of negotiation and conflict resolution. *Getting to Yes* offers a proven, step-by-step strategy for coming to mutually acceptable agreements in every sort of conflict. It offers readers a straightforward, universally applicable method for negotiating personal and professional disputes without getting angry or getting taken.

- Gladwell, Malcolm. *Blink: Thinking without Thinking.* (Little, Brown and Company, 2005.) *Blink* is about how we think without thinking, about choices that seem to be made in an instant—in the blink of an eye—that actually aren't as simple as they seem. Why are some people brilliant decision makers while others are consistently inept? Why do some people follow their instincts and win, while others end up stumbling into error? How do our brains really work—in the office, in the classroom, in the kitchen, and in the bedroom? And why are the best decisions often those that are impossible to explain to others?

- Haley, Jay. *Uncommon Therapy: The Psychiatric Techniques of Milton H. Erickson, M.D.* (W.W. Norton & Company, 1993.) Milton H. Erickson, M.D. is generally acknowledged to have been the world's leading practitioner of medical hypnosis. His "strategic therapy," using hypnotic techniques with or without actually inducing trance, allows him to get directly to the core of a problem and prescribe a course of action that can lead to rapid recovery. This book provides a comprehensive look at Dr. Erickson's theories in practice, through a series of case studies covering the kinds of problems that are likely to occur at various stages of the human life cycle.

- Halvorson, Heidi Grant. *Succeed: How We Can Reach Our Goals.* (Penguin Group, 2011.) And "You Are Probably Wrong About You." (Harvard Business Review, July 30, 2012.) Even very smart, very accomplished people are very bad at understanding why they succeed or fail. In *Succeed*, award-winning social psychologist Heidi Grant Halvorson offers counterintuitive insights, illuminating stories, and science-based information that can help anyone: Set a goal to pursue even in the face of adversity, build willpower, which can be strengthened like a muscle and avoid the kind of positive thinking that makes people fail. Whether you want to motivate your kids, your employees, or just yourself, *Succeed* unlocks the secrets of achievement, and shows you how to create new possibilities in every area of your life.

- Haney, C., Banks, W. C., & Zimbardo, P. G. (*Naval Research Review*, 30, 4-17, 1973.) Stanford prison experiment (SPE) was a study of the psychological effects of becoming a prisoner or prison guard. The experiment was conducted at Stanford University from August 14–20, 1971, by a team of researchers led by psychology professor Philip Zimbardo. It was funded by the US Office of Naval Research and was of interest to both the US Navy and Marine Corps as an investigation into the causes of conflict between military guards and prisoners.

- Lee, Harper. *To Kill a Mockingbird.* (Grand Central Publishing, 1982.) *To Kill a Mockingbird* became both an instant bestseller and a critical success when it was first published in 1960. It is the novel of a childhood in a sleepy Southern town and the crisis of conscience that rocked it. It went on to win the Pulitzer Prize in 1961 and was later made into an Academy Award–winning film, also a classic. This novel takes readers to the roots of human behavior—to innocence and experience, kindness and cruelty, love and hatred, humor and pathos.

- Mooyaart, B. M. (Translator), Frank, Anne. *Anne Frank: The Diary of a Young Girl.* (Bantam Books, a division of Random House, 1993.) Discovered in the attic in which she spent the last years of her life, Anne Frank's remarkable diary is a powerful reminder of the horrors of war and an eloquent testament to the human spirit. In 1942, with Nazis occupying Holland, a thirteen-year-old Jewish girl and her family fled their home in Amsterdam and went into hiding. For the next two years, until their whereabouts were betrayed to the Gestapo, they and another family lived cloistered in the "Secret Annex" of an old office building. Cut off from the outside world, they faced hunger, boredom, the constant cruelties of living in confined quarters, and the ever-present threat of discovery and death. In her diary Anne Frank recorded vivid impressions of her experiences during this period.

- O'Connor, Joseph and Seymour, John. *Introducing NLP: Psychological Skills for Understanding and Influencing People.* (Conari Press, 1993.) This book is an introduction and guide to the field known as Neuro-Linguistic Programming, or NLP. NLP is the art and science of excellence, derived from studies how top people in different fields obtain their outstanding results. These communication skills can be learned by anyone to improve their effectiveness both personally and professionally. The book describes many of the models of excellence that NLP has built in the fields of communication, business, education, and therapy.

- Pennebaker, James W. *Writing to Heal: A Guided Journal for Recovering from Trauma and Emotional Upheaval.* (New Harbinger, 2004.) The simple act of expressing your thoughts and feelings about emotionally challenging experiences on paper is proven to speed your recovery and improve your mental and physical health. Written by one of America's most distinguished research psychologists, this book guides you through a brief, powerful series of directed writing exercises you can do right in the book. Each will leave you with a stronger sense of value in the world and the ability to accept that life can be good—even when it is sometimes bad.

- Shaara, Michael. *The Killer Angels: The Classic Novel of the Civil War.* (Crown Publishers, 1974.) In the four most bloody and courageous days of our nation's history, two armies fought for two conflicting dreams. One dreamed of freedom, the other of a way of life. Far more than rifles and bullets were carried into battle. There were memories. There were promises. There was love. And far more than men fell on those Pennsylvania fields. Bright futures, untested innocence, and pristine beauty were also the casualties of war. Michael Shaara's Pulitzer Prize–winning masterpiece is unique, sweeping, and unforgettable—the dramatic story of the battleground for America's destiny.

- Wilson, Timothy D. *Strangers to Ourselves: Discovering the Adaptive Unconscious.* (Pages, 23, 34, Cambridge, Massachusetts: The Belknap press of Harvard University press, 2002 by the President and Fellows of Harvard College.) In a tour of the unconscious, Dr. Wilson introduces us to a hidden mental world of judgments, feelings, and motives that introspection may never show us. The adaptive unconscious that empirical psychology has revealed, and that Wilson describes, is much more than a repository of primitive drives and conflict-ridden memories. It is a set of pervasive, sophisticated mental processes that size up our worlds, set goals, and initiate action, all while we are consciously thinking about something else.

"The past cannot be changed, only one's views and interpretations of it, and even these change with the passage of time. Hence, at best, views and interpretations of the past are of importance only when they stultify the person into rigidity. Life is lived in the present for the morrow. Hence, psychotherapy is properly oriented about life today in preparation for tomorrow, next month, next year, the future, which in itself will compel many changes in the functioning of the person at all levels of his behavior."

~ Milton H. Erickson

Made in the USA
Middletown, DE
25 January 2015